THE EDIBLE WILD

To my father, Hjalmar Berglund, who first introduced to me the wonders of the outdoors and many of its wild edible plants; and to the Ontario Federation of Anglers and Hunters.

THE EDIBLE WILD

*A Complete Cookbook and Guide to Edible Wild Plants
in Canada and North America*

By
Berndt Berglund
and
Clare E. Bolsby

Illustrated by E. B. Sanders

PAGURIAN PRESS

CHARLES SCRIBNER'S SONS
NEW YORK

A — 1.72[M]

Printed in the United States of America
Library of Congress Catalog Card Number 78-162948
SBN 684-12601-X (trade cloth)
SBN 684-12759-8 (trade paper, SL)

CONTENTS

PREFACE

Included in this book are over fifty wild plants, trees and shrubs found growing in North America that provide edible food. These are only a few of thousands that grow in our bush, but we have selected the plants used most often by Indians and early settlers in this country.

Today, when more and more people are using the outdoors for recreation, tremendous interest is developing in the wild plants growing around us.

The gathering of wild foods is both fun and educational, and will enhance the eye and taste appeal of your menus. With pollution clouds hanging over us, it is a great relief to be able to gather fresh, unpolluted wild plants and roots.

Collecting these plants is not difficult. Many of them grow in your own backyard or in almost any rural area. There is no need to take long and expensive trips far into the woods to acquire wild fruits and vegetables for your dinner.

Unusual dishes will intrigue your friends, and even a connoisseur will have to admit he's seldom had meals as delightful as those made with the wild plants that we normally call weeds.

Because of their longer growing time, in most cases wild plants contain many, many times the vitamin content of fruits and vegetables we get from the garden. For instance, the dandelion has twenty-five times more vitamin A than tomato juice, and fifty times more than asparagus. The pulp of the rose hip has twenty-four times more vitamin C than orange juice. With just a little knowledge of Mother Nature's pantry, you could live well and stay healthy even if you were isolated in the bush.

This book is designed primarily for those who have never used wild plants for food and whose knowledge of these plants is small. At the same time, the authors have kept in mind the average outdoorsman and woman, who will find advice or suggestions that will be helpful.

Most wild plants are edible, but a few are poisonous. The most common of these are illustrated in this book. The ability to identify them is all-important.

With very few exceptions, the best outdoorsmen in the world have taught themselves to benefit from wild fruits and vegetables. They began as youngsters, many of them getting their first introduction to wild edible plants through the Scout movement or by imitating Indians or trappers. Interested in game and wild plants as most outdoorsmen are, it becomes natural for them not only to identify the plants but also their uses. A thorough knowledge of wild plants is basic for successful outdoor cooking.

Many of the recipes used in this handbook have been adapted from those of the pioneers and early settlers. Others came from the Indians. Since the eighteenth century, lovers of nature in North America have been experimenting with new and imaginative ways of bringing wild bounty to the table for their delight.

This unique guide and cookbook for the edible wild plants in Canada and North America will be as valuable to the hunter in the bush as to the gourmet in his own kitchen.

NOTES ON THE RECIPES

The liquid quart measure used in these recipes is the 40-ounce Imperial quart, which is the equivalent of 5 cups.

If you have no kitchen scales, a bathroom scale is adequate for weighing wild fruits and vegetables where measurement is by weight.

All recipes, with the exception of beverages, serve 6.

BLACK MUSTARD

(Brassica nigra)

These plants are annuals, often reaching 4 to 6 feet in height. They may be simple branching plants, with the lower part of the stem having stiff hairs, while the upper part may be smooth.

All the leaves have stalks, and the lower are large and deeply lobed, but the upper leaves are small and merely toothed. The flowers are in long racemes and yellow. The seed pods are four-angled and stand erect to the stem.

This plant is a native of Eurasia but is common all over the northern part of the United States and Canada. It is universally recognized because of its bright yellow flowers, which give fields the look of having been painted with gold.

BLACK MUSTARD

The name mustard is a corruption of the name "must seeds" given the seeds by ancient Britons at the time of the Roman occupation. To make a condiment, the Romans used to grind the seeds and mix them with new wine or "must".

IN THE BUSH

As a Fresh Vegetable: Young mustard plants are most agreeable to eat raw. They will give a real lift when you are tired and dehydrated after coming back to camp from a spring hunting or fishing trip.

In Soup: Early in the season I like the black mustard best in a cream of mustard leaves soup with wild leek. One simple method of making it is to heat a quart of milk slowly, almost to the boiling point. Meanwhile melt 2 tablespoons of bacon fat in the frying pan and add a couple of wild onions, finely chopped. Let the onions brown for a minute or so before you add a couple of cups of finely shredded mustard leaves and a pinch of salt and pepper. If I have a couple of tablespoons of flour, I add them to thicken the soup. Cook for about 5 minutes, then add 1 cup of the heated milk with constant stirring and simmer for a couple of minutes. Then add the mixture from the frying pan. Mix well, and I am telling you, this is a mouth-tingling soup.

With Fish: If you are far from camp and all the conveniences, you can simply stuff your fish with black mustard leaves. Using a snare wire as kitchen string, sew or wrap up the fish, and then bury it in the coals for a couple of hours. This way, you have a fish and green dish at the same time.

As a Cooked Vegetable: Later in the summer, the profusion of golden flowers can be capitalized upon to make a colorful and vitamin-rich dish. Pick the flowers, remembering you need a lot. Plunge them into boiling water and let them cook for 3 minutes. Remove from heat and let stand for 10 minutes, well covered. Drain and spread with melted butter or margarine or even with porcupine fat.

In Salad: There is nothing that will surpass black mustard seeds to garnish or season the fresh green salads which we so highly prize in the spring.

HOME RECIPES
CREAM OF MUSTARD SOUP

1½ pounds fresh young mustard leaves	6 cups chicken stock
1 tablespoon mustard seed	3 egg yolks
6 tablespoons butter	1 cup heavy cream
6 tablespoons flour	1 teaspoon salt
	½ teaspoon white pepper

Clean and wash the freshly picked black mustard leaves under cold running water and drain on paper towels. Crush the mustard seeds and set aside.

In a heavy 3 to 4-quart saucepan, melt 4 tablespoons butter over high heat. When it gives off a nutty odor, lower the heat. Remove the pan from the heat and stir in the flour, return and cook for 5 minutes, stirring constantly until the roux is smooth and creamy.

Remove from heat and let stand for a minute. Stir in the chicken stock, beating constantly with a wire whisk. Return to heat, and stir until thick and perfectly smooth. Add the mustard leaves, saving out a few for garnish, and the crushed mustard seeds. Cook over low heat for 25 minutes.

Purée the soup through a food mill into a mixing bowl and then again through a fine sieve back into the saucepan. With a wire whisk, blend the egg yolks and the cream. Whisk in a cupful of the hot puréed soup a little at a time, and then reverse the operation by whisking the egg mixture into the soup. Bring the soup almost to a boil and simmer for 3 minutes.

Taste and season the soup with salt and pepper, add a few shredded mustard leaves and 2 tablespoons of soft butter.

Serve in individual serving bowls.

FRIED TROUT IN MUSTARD AND SOUR CREAM SAUCE

4 fresh trout, ½ pound each	3 cups fresh mustard leaves
½ cup flour	2 tablespoons soft butter
1 teaspoon salt	1 cup sour cream
Pepper	1 tablespoon crushed mustard
6 tablespoons butter	seeds

Wash and clean the fish under running water, pat them dry inside and out with paper towels and sprinkle a little salt inside each fish. Spread the flour on a piece of wax paper and sprinkle the salt and pepper evenly over the flour. Roll the fish around in the flour and shake off any excess.

In a heavy 12-inch skillet melt the butter over high heat. When it gives off a nutty odor, lower the heat a little and fry the trout. The fish should not have more than 3 minutes on each side. Two fish is enough to take care of at one time. When the fish is golden brown and flaky, remove from the skillet with tongs, trying not to break the golden skin. When all the trout have been browned, keep them warm in a 200° oven.

Place the mustard leaves and the mustard seeds into the fat in which you fried the fish and cook for 8 minutes. Drain on paper towels. Pour off the fat from the skillet and replace with soft butter. Stir over low heat, scraping up the brown pan drippings with a wooden spoon. Add the sour cream and continue to stir for 3 minutes, then add the mustard leaves. Mix well so all the leaves are coated on all sides. Taste for seasoning.

Remove the fish from the oven. Place them on a heated serving platter and pour the sauce all around the fish.

Serve at once.

MUSTARD LEAVES AND LAMB CASSEROLE

3½ pounds lamb	1½ cups chopped wild onion
2 tablespoons butter	2 tablespoons salt
½ cup flour	¼ teaspoon pepper
2 pounds mustard leaves	2½ cups beef stock
2 tablespoons mustard seed	

Preheat the oven to 375°. Trim fat from lamb and cut in 2-inch cubes. In a heavy 12-inch skillet melt the butter over high heat. When it gives off a nutty odor, lower the heat and add the cubed lamb. Cook until well browned on all sides, then using tongs, remove from the skillet to a large mixing bowl.

Sprinkle the flour over the meat and stir with a wooden spoon until it is evenly coated and there is no trace of flour left.

Using a 5-quart casserole equipped with a lid, arrange a layer of the browned meat on the bottom, cover with a layer of mustard leaves, sprinkle with half the mustard seeds, onion, salt and pepper. Repeat, ending with a layer of mustard leaves.

Place the skillet in which you browned the meat over medium heat and let the drippings come to a boil. Add the beef stock and boil, stirring all the time to remove any brown bits from the bottom and sides of the skillet.

Pour the liquid over the meat and mustard leaves in the casserole. Sprinkle salt and pepper on top and bake for 1½ hours in the oven, or until the meat is tender when pierced with the tip of a sharp knife.

Serve from the casserole.

BLACK TABLE MUSTARD

2 cups black mustard seeds　　**4 tablespoons rum**
1 cup superfine sugar　　**2 tablespoons heavy cream**

Grind the mustard seeds finely. If you are in camp, use two flat stones; if at home, use the food blender. I usually place the seeds between two pieces of wax paper on a hard surface and using a bottle, crush down hard on the seeds. This should produce a fine powder.

Place the crushed mustard seeds in a small bowl. Add the sugar and stir well. Add the rum and the heavy cream and stir until you have a smooth paste. If the paste is too thick, add a tablespoon of white vinegar, or thin to your taste. Let me tell you, this mustard is hot.

Place the mustard in a jar with a tight lid and remove only as much as you need at a time. The mustard improves with age.

BULRUSH

(Scirpus validus and acutus)

The bulrush is a tall, light green, soft-fleshed marsh plant. Its spikelets are either solitary or in groups, and are very commonly umbelled. This plant is very often found in or around marshes and lakesides, where it rises conspicuously out of shallow water. The bulrush is a year-round source of food. The rootstalk is available from fall to spring. The young leading tip from which next years shoot will emerge can be eaten in the fall when it is crisp and sweet.

BULRUSH

IN THE BUSH

As a Fresh Vegetable: The young shoots and the tender parts inside the base of the stalks are edible raw or when boiled or added to stews. The young base roots are also edible raw or cooked.

ROASTED BULRUSH ROOTS

Dig up the roots and clean thoroughly, removing all hair roots by scraping, then wrap in big leaves. Dig a hole in the ground about 18 inches across and 6 inches deep. In it build a fire. When you have a good bed of coals, remove most of the coals from the hole and place the wrapped roots in, then scrape the coals back on top of the roots.

Roast for 2 to 3 hours.

BULRUSH STEW

Peel the skin off the roots and cut in inch-long pieces. Place in a pot with boiling water, add a few wild onions or sprigs of mint. Then add pieces of porcupine or other small animals that you have on hand.

Boil for one hour and you will have a very tasty stew.

BULRUSH FLOUR

Clean the roots thoroughly. Dry them completely in a dry place or in the sun and then remove the fibers from the root. Pound the remaining pulp into a flour.

The texture of the flour, of course, depends upon the energy expended in its preparation. It is very sweet to taste.

Flour can also be made by boiling the roots into a starchy gruel and then letting the water evaporate in the sun or at the fireside.

BULRUSH PANCAKES

Peel the skin from the roots, cut into small sections, add water and boil to a gruel. Cool. Stir into the gruel porcupine fat or any other fat, then add chopped porcupine or bacon. Heat a couple of flat stones over the fire, form small patties of the mixture and fry on the stones.

If berries are in season, mash a cupful and use as a complement.

BULRUSH BREAD

Skin the roots and cut them into small pieces, then boil to a gruel. Remove the fibers and let the water evaporate from the gruel. When all the water is gone you will have a fine sweet-tasting flour. Mix some fat into the flour, roll out on a flat stone, and bake in a reflector oven. Or make small rolls, about 6 inches long and half an inch thick, twist around a stick and set in front of the fire to bake.

SUGAR SUBSTITUTE

Indians in the part of the continent where no maple was found used to make a weak sugar substitute by boiling bulrush roots from 7 to 15 hours.

Clean the roots and bruise them thoroughly. Add water and boil down the liquid to whatever thickness is desired.

HOME RECIPES

BULRUSH BROTH

1½ pounds oxtail, cut up
1½ teaspoons salt
2 tablespoons bulrush flour
2 tablespoons bacon fat
6 cups water
½ cup bulrush shoots

3 wild onions
¼ cup wild rice
3 bulrush roots, thinly sliced
1 tablespoon Worcestershire
   sauce

Roll the meat pieces in a mixture of flour and salt. Sauté in hot fat, turning several times to brown completely. Add the water, bulrush shoots and wild onions, then cover and simmer 1½ hours. Uncover and add remaining ingredients. Cook slowly for another 1½ hours or until the wild rice is tender. Stir occasionally and add a little water if necessary. Taste for seasoning.

DELUXE BULRUSH CASSEROLE

1 pound small bulrush sprouts
1 pound ground beef
1 large onion
   Salt and pepper

1 can tomato soup
1 cup tomato juice
   Potato chips

The small inner stalks of the bulrush are tender and taste like asparagus when cooked. These stalks are easy to remove from the plant if you part the leaves and pull the shoots from the roots. Wash them in running water, cut in small pieces and soak in salted water.

Mix meat and finely chopped onion, add salt and pepper to taste. In a greased casserole put a layer of bulrush sprouts, then a layer of meat. Repeat until all the ingredients are used, then pour tomato soup on top.

Place in a 425° oven for about an hour or until the bulrush sprouts are tender. Add a little tomato juice from time to time. Top with potato chips and let stand in oven 10 minutes more. Serve hot from casserole.

CREAMED BULRUSH

12 ounces tender bulrush shoots
½ teaspoon salt
1 cup water
3 tablespoons butter
3 tablespoons bulrush flour

3 cups liquid (milk plus drained
   bulrush juice)
1 tablespoon sugar
¼ teaspoon pepper
   Hard-cooked egg slices

Rinse the fresh bulrush shoots and steam with salt and water in a covered pan until limp. Drain off all juice into a measuring cup and save.

Chop bulrush shoots finely. Melt butter in the top of a double boiler and stir in flour, gradually add bulrush juice and enough milk to bring total liquid to 3 cups. Stir constantly until smooth, and season, adding more salt if necessary. Heat thoroughly.

Garnish each serving with hard-cooked egg slices. Goes well with any smoked fish dish.

BEEF STEW WITH WILD VEGETABLES

4 tablespoons butter	¾ cup bulrush shoots, cut finely
3 pounds boneless beef, cut in 2-inch chunks	½ cup finely chopped wild leek
	3 cups beef stock
3 tablespoons flour	1 cup finely chopped bulrush root
1 teaspoon salt	4 parsley sprigs, 1 leek (white
Pepper	part), 1 bay leaf, tied together
½ cup fresh mint	Vegetable garnish

Preheat the oven to 450°. In a heavy 10 to 12-inch skillet heat 2 table-spoons of butter to the point where it gives off a nutty smell. Brown the beef chunks a few at a time, taking care not to crowd the skillet. When the chunks are well browned on all sides, remove them with a slotted spoon to a Dutch oven or a heavy 6 to 8-quart casserole. Pour off almost all the fat from the skillet and set aside.

Sprinkle the browned beef with flour, salt and pepper, adding the finely chopped mint. Turn the meat around in the casserole in order to coat the beef as evenly as possible. Place the casserole in the middle of the oven uncovered and cook the beef, turning it every few minutes or until there are no traces of gummy flour. Remove the casserole from the oven and set aside. Reduce the heat to 300°.

To the fat in the skillet add the remaining butter and melt over high heat. When the butter gives off a nutty odor, lower the heat, add the chopped bulrush shoots and wild leek, and cook 3 to 4 minutes, stirring constantly. Pour in the beef stock and bring to a boil, scraping in any bits and pieces that cling to the sides of the skillet. Add the bulrush root, stir once more, and cook for 8 to 10 minutes. Add the mixture to the browned beef in the casserole, stir gently with a wooden spoon and add the parsley sprigs, leek and bay leaf.

Bring the casserole to a boil on top of the stove, cover tightly and place it in the middle of the oven to simmer for one hour.

VEGETABLE GARNISH

12 to 15 wild onions	6 to 8 bulrush roots
10 to 12 arrowhead tubers	½ pound green beans, cut in inch
6 medium dandelion roots	lengths
6 tablespoons butter	2 tablespoons fresh parsley
1 pound fresh green peas	

Peel the wild onion and set aside. In a 3 to 4-quart saucepan put the cleaned arrowhead tubers and the dandelion roots. Add a pinch of salt and cover with water, bring to a boil and cook for 20 minutes. Drain water from vegetables and set aside until cool enough to remove skins, making sure they are skinned as thinly as possible. Cut the dandelion roots in 2-inch cylinders or olive shapes.

In a heavy 10 to 12-inch skillet melt butter over high heat. When there is a slight nutty odor, reduce the heat and add the wild onions, bulrush roots, dandelion roots and the arrowhead tubers. Cook over moderate heat for 15 minutes or until lightly browned, stirring from time to time to ensure that vegetables are well coated with butter.

Bring 2 quarts of water to a boil in a 3 to 4-quart saucepan, add the fresh peas and beans and boil them briskly for 6 to 8 minutes. Drain in a sieve and then plunge the sieve under cold running water for a minute or so. Set aside.

After the beef has cooked for an hour, remove the casserole from the oven and strain the entire contents through a large sieve into a large mixing bowl. While the braising liquid is draining wash the casserole dish and spread the onions, bulrush roots, dandelion roots and the arrowhead tubers in the bottom. With tongs pick the pieces of beef out of the sieve and arrange over the vegetables. Skim off the fat in the mixing bowl and taste the sauce for seasoning, then pour it over the meat and vegetables in the casserole.

Bring to a boil over medium heat on top of the stove, cover tightly and return to the oven for about 15 minutes longer, or until the beef and vegetables are tender.

This dish is served from the casserole, garnished with chopped parsley.

BULRUSH AND PARTRIDGE RAGOUT SOUP

1 to 1½ pounds partridge parts (necks, wings, backs, giblets)	½ cup finely chopped bulrush root
1 small veal knuckle (about ½ pound)	½ cup diced dandelion roots
8 peppercorns	½ cup finely chopped wild onion
1 teaspoon salt	½ cup diced bulrush shoots
2½ quarts chicken stock	2 tablespoons flour
4 tablespoons butter	3 tablespoons finely chopped mint

Skin and draw the partridge, wash thoroughly and pat dry. Cut into small pieces. In a 4 to 5-quart soup kettle combine the partridge parts, veal knuckle, peppercorns, salt and chicken stock (add water if needed to cover by an inch). Bring to a boil over high heat, skimming the scum from the surface as it rises. Partly cover the pan and reduce heat to a slow simmer for 1½ to 2 hours.

In a 2 to 3-quart saucepan put the bulrush roots, dandelion roots, salt and water to cover. Bring to the boil, lower heat and cook for 30 minutes. Drain and set aside to cool, then dice the dandelion roots in ¼-inch pieces and peel and chop the bulrush roots and shoots.

In a 10 to 12-inch skillet melt the butter over high heat. When it gives off a nutty odor, lower the heat and add the wild onion. Cook for 4 to 5 minutes then add the diced dandelion roots, bulrush roots and shoots. Stir gently to cover the vegetables with butter, cover the skillet and cook over low heat for 20 minutes. Check the skillet occasionally and if necessary, add a tablespoon of chicken stock to keep vegetables moist.

After 2 hours pour the soup through a large sieve into a large mixing bowl. Remove all edible pieces of the partridge and dice coarsely. Discard veal bones and peppercorns. Return the stock to a large casserole, skim off as much fat from the surface as you can, and bring to a simmer again.

Remove skillet from the heat and sprinkle the flour over the vegetables. Stir together until all the flour is absorbed, then stir in 2 cups of the partridge stock and return to heat, stirring constantly. Cook for 10 minutes or until the stock is smooth and thick.

Pour the contents of the skillet into the simmering partridge stock, using a wire whisk to beat the creamy mixture and stock together. Add the partridge and bring the soup almost to a boil, reduce the heat, and simmer partly covered for 10 minutes. Taste for seasoning.

Pour the soup into individual serving bowls and sprinkle with chopped mint.

HUNTERS' STEW WITH BULRUSHES

2 cups finely chopped wild onion	½ cup dry red wine
2 medium-sized bulrush roots	1 teaspoon salt
10 slices of bacon, diced	½ teaspoon black pepper
3 pounds boneless beef chunk, cut into 2-inch cubes	1 cup wild rice
	8 bulrush shoots
1 tablespoon finely chopped chives	1½ cups beef stock
	Parsley and leeks for garnish
2 cups water	

Skin the onion, chop very fine, and put aside. In a 2-quart saucepan cover the bulrush roots with water, add a pinch of salt, and bring to a boil. Reduce heat and cook for 30 minutes.

Drain water, scrape and slice bulrush roots in ¼-inch slices and set aside.

In a 12-inch skillet cook the bacon over medium heat for 10 minutes or until most of the fat is rendered and it is slightly crisp. Remove bacon with a slotted spoon and set aside. Pour off all fat but a thin film and set aside.

Add the onions and bring the heat up. Cook until the onions are transparent. Add the beef cubes and the rendered bacon fat, then the chives and the bulrush roots. Cook for 15 minutes over medium heat. Return the bacon to the skillet, stir in the water and the wine, season with salt and pepper, reduce the heat to a low simmer, cover and cook about an hour.

Drop wild rice into a quart saucepan. Add a pinch of salt and just enough water to cover. Bring to a boil, lower heat and cook for 30 minutes.

Gradually stir the cooked rice, bulrush shoots and 1 cup of beef stock into the skillet. Bring to a boil, reduce heat, cover and simmer for 30 minutes.

Taste for seasoning. If rice becomes too dry, add remaining beef stock to keep it from sticking to the bottom of the pan.

Serve this dish from a deep serving bowl and garnish with finely chopped leeks and parsley.

CATTAIL

(Typha latifolia)

The cattail can be identified by its tall, firm stalks, tipped with an interesting flower structure composed of a dense spike. The leaves are somewhat sword shaped, and the bases of the leaves are often submerged. When the flowers fall off they leave a dark brown spike.

CATTAIL

The cattail grows in marshy places and like the bulrush, is a source of food all year round.

IN THE BUSH

As a Cooked Vegetable: The inner stalks, after cleaning, are excellent in stews or boiled in salted water. The roots are edible cooked or roasted after they have been scraped, cleaned and sliced.

As a Gruel: Scrape and clean the roots, cut into small pieces, remove the fibers, add a little water, and boil into a thick gruel.

As Meal: Dry the root thoroughly, skin, remove fibers and pound into meal.

The pollen of the plant is delicious either eaten raw or ground to flour. It resembles musty wheat in flavor. The Indians used the pollen to make bread or cakes.

Pollen was also used by the Indians to flavor and thicken soups.

As a Fire Starter: In New Zealand the pollen is widely used for tinder, since it is very inflammable.

As Bedding: An old shirt with sleeves tied together and filled with cattail pollen makes a wonderful pillow for an emergency bed.

STEAMED CATTAIL ROOTS

Pull up the root, clean, scrape, and remove root hairs. Wrap in large leaves.

Dig a shallow pit and line with flat stones. Place over them a good bed of coals from your main fire, and feed the coals with small branches to get the stones as hot as possible. Scrape the coals out of the pit and replace them with wet green grass. Place the cattail roots, wrapped in leaves, on the grass and cover with a second layer of grass, then earth. Punch a hole down to the food level and pour in a small quantity of water, then block the hole with earth and leave undisturbed for an hour or more to let the steam cook the food.

CATTAIL SOUP

For the lone survivor without cooking utensils, it seems to be impossible to make soup without a pot of some kind. But you can make an excellent pot out of birch bark. Form the birch bark into a funnel and put a stopper in the small hole in the bottom with clay or a small stone sealed with clay.

If you remember to keep the water level higher in the funnel than the surrounding coal bed, the birch bark will not burn.

As for the soup, fill the funnel three-quarters full of water and add some of the dark meat from a squirrel that has been properly skinned and cut up in small pieces. Simmer for half an hour, then add two handfuls of pollen from the cattail. Simmer for another half hour and you will have a wonderful soup.

CATTAIL BREAD

Collect the pollen from the cattail by bending the stem over a pot or funnel of birch bark. Hit the spike hard and the pollen will fall out. Grind the

12

pollen between two stones to a fine flour. Mix the flour with a bit of porcupine fat and water and make balls of the mixture. Flatten the balls into cakes and griddle in a reflector oven made out of flat stones.

HOME RECIPES

CATTAIL STEW

2 pounds boned breast and shoulder of mutton	Salt and pepper
2 pounds cattail root	1 bunch fresh mint
8 medium-sized wild onions	3 cups water

Cut the mutton into small pieces and set aside. Wash the cattail root, remove root hairs and cut into ¼-inch slices. Clean the wild onion and slice ¼ inch thick.

Take a 3-quart saucepan or better still, an old iron pot (everything tastes better cooked in an iron pot). Line the bottom with a layer of meat. Season with salt and pepper. On top of the meat put a layer of sliced cattail root, and a layer of sliced onion on top of the roots.

Repeat the operation until all the ingredients are used. Put a large bunch of mint in the middle.

Moisten with water, and cook gently over low heat for two hours. The cattail root serves a double purpose in this dish: to give the stew flavor, and to thicken it.

This dish is best served boiling hot.

CATTAIL HAM UNDER ASHES

2 to 3-pound cottage roll, cured and precooked	1¼ cups water
1 pound cattail flour	1 pound soft butter
½ teaspoon salt	1 egg yolk
	Port

Place the cottage roll in water to cover and poach for 20 minutes.

While it simmers crush the pollen of the cattail to a flour consistency and put on a mixing board. Make a hollow in the middle of the flour and pour all the salt and water into it. Mix without kneading. Put the paste together and let rest for 10 minutes in a cold place. Puff paste should be done with the smallest amount of kneading possible.

Spread the prepared paste on a flour-dusted board in the shape of a thin cake. Spread the soft butter over it without completely covering the paste; draw the edges of the paste towards the center, so it will cover the butter and form a square. Leave to rest for 10 minutes and then begin to work the paste, rolling it out to the length of a foot and keeping it 1 inch thick.

Fold the paste in thirds and roll it down with the rolling pin. Do this operation 3 times. Ten minutes after the last rolling the paste is ready to be used.

Drain the poached cottage roll and remove all strings and fat. Sprinkle the ham with sugar and put under the grill for five minutes to glaze it.

Preheat oven to 400°. Roll out the paste large enough to completely enclose the ham. Place it with the glazed side down on the paste.

Draw the ends of the paste together and seal them with a little water. Make sure the ham is completely enclosed. Place it with the sealed side of the paste down on the pan. Brush with egg yolk, make a slit on the top for the steam to escape, and bake until the paste is dry and well browned.

When you take the ham out of the oven, make a hole in the pastry and pour in a glass of port.

Serve hot with fiddleheads.

CATTAIL PANCAKES FILLED WITH BLUEBERRIES

1 cup cattail flour	6 tablespoons butter, melted
3 eggs	½ teaspoon salt
2 cups milk or 1 cup milk and 1 cup light cream	Blueberry filling

To make cattail flour, boil the root stalks into a starchy gruel and dry in a 175° oven. After the gruel is dry, remove the long fibrous hairs and you have flour.

Combine the eggs with ½ cup of milk and beat for 2 or 3 minutes with a rotary beater or whisk. Add the cattail flour all at once and beat to a heavy smooth consistency. Beat in the remaining milk and then the melted butter and salt. Batter is very thin.

A heavy cast-iron skillet should be used. Grease lightly with pastry brush or paper towel dipped in a little clarified butter. Because of the large amount of butter in the batter, the skillet will require little if any additional grease.

When the skillet is so hot that a few drops of water flicked on its surface bounce around and evaporate instantly, drop 1 tablespoon of batter onto the pan for each pancake. They should form 3-inch circles.

When the edges brown lightly after about a minute, turn the pancakes with a narrow spatula and cook another minute or two.

BLUEBERRY FILLING

3 cups fresh blueberries	½ cup sugar

Crush the berries slightly and sprinkle with the sugar. Let stand for an hour or so.

Put 2 tablespoons of blueberries in the middle of each cooked pancake and roll it up, securing with a toothpick if necessary. Sprinkle lightly with sugar, set on a platter and keep warm in a 200° oven while you complete the rest.

These pancakes are best served "from pan to plate".

CATTAIL BREAD

1½ cups cattail flour	1 package active yeast
1½ teaspoons salt	1 teaspoon sugar
1 cup boiling water	¼ cup lukewarm water
2 tablespoons butter	2 cups all purpose flour

Scrape and clean several cattail roots, place them on a cookie sheet and put in the oven under low heat. Let stand overnight to dry. Then skin the roots and remove the fibers. Using a blender, pulverize the roots until fine. Let stand for a day in a dry place such as a cold oven.

In a large mixing bowl, combine 1 cup of cattail meal, the salt and boiling water. Stir vigorously until smooth. In a small saucepan melt the butter. Stir 1 tablespoon into the dough.

In a small bowl sprinkle the yeast and sugar over the lukewarm water. Let stand for 5 minutes, then stir to dissolve yeast completely. Place the bowl in a draft-free oven for 10 minutes, or until the yeast has doubled its volume.

Mix the yeast into the dough, stirring constantly, and add the rest of the cattail flour and 1 cup of all purpose flour. Make a ball of the dough, place in a bowl, cover with a towel, and place it in a draft-free corner for about 30 minutes or until it has doubled in volume.

With a pastry brush, coat the bottom and sides of a 9-inch pie plate with the remaining butter. Turn the dough out on a lightly floured surface and punch down. Knead the dough for about 5 minutes, adding 1 cup of flour to make it stiff. Shape it into a round flat cake and place it in the greased pan. Cover with a towel and set aside in a warm place for about 30 minutes or until it has doubled in volume.

Preheat the oven to 375°. Bake the bread in the middle of the oven for 45 minutes or until the top is golden. Transfer to a rack to cool.

CATTAIL PANCAKES FILLED WITH APPLES

FILLING

3 pounds crabapples or wild apples	4 tablespoons sugar
	2 tablespoons ground cinnamon
6 tablespoons butter	

Peel and core the apples and slice into ¼-inch wedges. In a heavy 12-inch skillet, melt the butter over high heat. When it gives off a nutty odor, reduce the heat and drop the apple slices into the skillet.

In a small mixing bowl, mix the sugar and cinnamon thoroughly. Sprinkle the mixture over the apples and cook, stirring gently from time to time. Set the skillet aside and let stand overnight.

PANCAKES

8 eggs	6 teaspoons sugar
2½ cups milk	½ teaspoon salt
1 cup cattail flour	6 tablespoons butter

Scrape and clean the cattail roots, place them on a cookie sheet and then into a 175° oven overnight. Skin the roots and remove the fibers. Using a blender, pulverize the roots until fine. Let stand for a day in a cold oven.

Preheat the broiler for 5 minutes. Combine the eggs and milk in a large mixing bowl and beat with a wire whisk. Mix the cattail flour with the sugar and salt and add to the egg and milk mixture a little at a time. Mix well.

Line a heavy 10-inch skillet with aluminum foil, being careful not to puncture the foil and bringing it all the way up the sides of the skillet. Place the skillet over moderate heat and melt a tablespoon of butter in the foil.

With a pastry brush grease the bottom and sides well and pour ½ cup of batter into the pan, tipping it from side to side to spread the batter evenly over the bottom. Spread ¾ of a cup of apples evenly over the batter and let the pancake cook for 3 to 4 minutes. Pour a second ½ cup of batter on top of the apples, covering them carefully.

Slide the skillet under the broiler and cook until the pancake is golden brown on top. To prevent burning, place the pancakes 7 to 8 inches from the element.

When cooked, place a large platter on top of the skillet and holding firmly to both, invert them together. The pancake should come out easily.

Remove the aluminum foil and put it back in the skillet, melt butter and proceed with the next pancake in the same manner as the first.

If you wish, just before serving sprinkle a teaspoon of sugar on each pancake.

CATTAIL BROWN SUGAR LOAF

4 packages active dry yeast	2 cups cattail root flour
3 teaspoons brown sugar	1½ cups all purpose flour
1¼ cups lukewarm water	1 tablespoon soft butter
1 tablespoon melted butter	

Scrape and clean some cattail roots. Place them on a cookie sheet in a 175° oven overnight to dry. Skin the roots and remove the fibers. Using a blender, pulverize the roots until fine. Let stand for a day in an cold oven.

Sprinkle the yeast and 1 teaspoon of the brown sugar over ¼ cup of the lukewarm water. Make sure the water is lukewarm. Let the mixture stand for 4 minutes, then stir to dissolve the yeast completely. Set the bowl in a warm, draft-free spot until the mixture starts to bubble and has doubled in size.

Pour the yeast mixture into a large mixing bowl, add the remaining water, and with a wooden spoon mix in the rest of the sugar, the melted butter, salt, white flour and 1½ cups of cattail flour. When the mixture forms a smooth dough, gather it into a ball, cover the bowl with a kitchen towel, and let it rest at room temperature for about 15 minutes.

Transfer the dough to a floured pastry board and knead until it is elastic and smooth. Use the extra ½ cup of cattail flour to sprinkle the dough or pastry board if either becomes sticky.

Gather the dough in a large ball, place in a lightly buttered mixing bowl, and cover with the kitchen towel. Let the dough rest in a warm, draft-free place for about an hour, or until it has doubled in volume.

Preheat oven to 375°. With a pastry brush lightly spread the remaining butter on a cookie sheet and sprinkle with flour. Knock the excess flour off the sheet by rapping it hard on the table top.

Punch the dough down with your fist and knead again briefly on the pastry board. Shape it into a round flat loaf about 10 to 12 inches in diameter, and set it on the cookie sheet.

Bake one hour, or until the bread has a dark brown crust and a toothpick inserted in the center comes out dry and clean.

If you wish to glaze the loaf, mix 1 teaspoon brown sugar and 2 table-spoons water and brush it on the minute the loaf comes out of the oven.

CATTAIL CRULLERS

2 cups water
1 teaspoon salt
2 cups cattail flour

Vegetable oil for deep frying
Honey

Scrape and clean several cattail roots. Put them on a cookie sheet in a 175° oven to dry overnight.

Skin the roots and remove the fibers. Using a blender, pulverise the roots until fine. Let the flour stand in a cold oven overnight to dry.

In a saucepan, bring the water and salt to a boil. Remove from heat and pour in all the flour. Beat with an electric beater until the mixture forms a thick paste. Cool to room temperature.

Heat 3 inches of oil in a deep fryer until it starts to smoke, or until the temperature is 400° on a thermometer.

Spoon out the dough onto a floured cookie sheet to form a cake ¼ inch thick. With a knife, make ribbons ½ inch wide and 6 inches long. Carefully lift ribbons into the hot fat. Fry for 5 to 8 minutes or until they are golden brown, turning at least once.

When cooked, drain on brown paper for a minute, then on a heated platter, and keep hot.

Before serving, pour a little honey along the top.

CHICKWEED

CHICKWEED

(Stellaria media)

The stem of this plant is weak and branched, with a hairy fringe. The leaves grow opposite each other on the stem. The flowers are white, somewhat star shaped, with heart-shaped petals. This plant stands about 12 inches in height and is a common weed in fields and meadows. It prefers moist soil. Chickweed is one of the plants from which seed food is obtained for pet birds.

IN THE BUSH

The greens can be eaten raw or cooked. Indians used the seeds for bread or to thicken soups. Early in the spring the leaves give the spring taste to a salad. However, I find that the leaves and the stems are best cooked, and can take the place of asparagus tips at any time.

Used as a potherb, chickweed gives a stew a taste like okra.

An old Indian friend maintains there is no wild green which can set off a stew of rabbit as well as chickweed can. Many a time when I was traveling in his company he made this dish for me.

RABBIT STEW WITH CHICKWEED

Skin the rabbit, cut it up into small pieces and place in a pot. Add a little water or if you have any sort of firewater, put in ½ cup. Cover tightly and simmer in the campfire for about 1 hour. Clean the chickweed and put 4 handfuls of plant leaves and stems into the pot. Simmer for a further ½ hour, and the stew is ready to eat.

HOME RECIPES

FRESH CHICKWEED SALAD

2 pounds young chickweed leaves
and stems
4 teaspoons soy sauce

2 teaspoons sugar
2 teaspoons vegetable oil

Clean and wash the leaves and stems under running water. Cut the chickweed into small serving pieces. Place a 2-quart saucepan over high heat, add 1 quart water and let it come to a boil. Add the chickweed leaves and boil rapidly for 2 minutes. Remove from the heat and drain at once. Run cold water over the chickweed leaves to stop the cooking and set the color. Drain on a double thickness of paper towel.

Using a small mixing bowl, combine the soy sauce, sugar and vegetable oil. Mix well or until the sugar is dissolved. Pat the chickweed leaves dry with paper towel and add to the oil mixture. With a large spoon toss the salad, making sure all the leaves are well coated with oil. Chill for at least 1 hour in the refrigerator before serving.

CHICKWEED PANCAKES

½ pound fresh chickweed leaves	1 teaspoon salt
1½ cups milk	1 cup flour
2 eggs	2 tablespoons butter, melted
1 teaspoon sugar	2 tablespoons soft butter

Clean and wash the chickweed leaves under running water, place in a 2-quart saucepan and cover with water. Place over high heat and boil for 3 minutes. Remove from heat and plunge into cold water. Drain on a double thickness of paper towel and pat dry. Chop the leaves finely and set aside.

Using a large mixing bowl, combine the milk, eggs, sugar, flour, salt and melted butter. Use an electric beater and mix at medium speed. When the ingredients are well mixed, stir in the chopped chickweed leaves.

Place a heavy 12-inch skillet over the heat and coat the surface with soft butter. When the skillet is very hot, drop in 2 tablespoons of batter and using a spoon, flatten out the pancake so it will form a 3-inch disk.

Fry the pancakes for about 3 minutes on each side. Place the finished pancakes on a hot plate in the oven until all the batter is used up. Serve with cranberry jelly.

COMMON PLANTAIN

(Plantago major)

The leaves of the common plantain are parallel-veined, soft and green in color. The seeds are green or brown and are small and closely packed towards the top of a single stem. The base of the leaf stem is sometimes pinkish in color.

The common plantain is an introduced weed that can be found all over the countryside as well as on the streets of a big city.

COMMON PLANTAIN

IN THE BUSH

Plantain leaves make an excellent green salad. As a matter of fact, the greener they are the more vitamin A and C they hold. Many a cook murders greens by overcooking. I learned a trick from an old Indian on cooking greens. The first time he watched me cook a potful, he said, "Don't you know the simplest way to cook all greens is to start them in a minimum amount of water and cook them, covered, as rapidly as possible?" All the cooking fluid should be used, as most of the minerals and vitamins are contained in the water. Personally, I prefer to drink the fluid or use it as the base for my sauce or gravy.

As a Cooked Vegetable: The young tender leaves should be plucked and stripped of bad parts and washed in salt water for 4 to 5 minutes. I prefer sugar instead of salt for cooking or even better, if I have wild honey, I mix it with the leaves when they are almost boiled.

As a Fresh Vegetable: Pick the young leaves, clean, and discard any brown parts. Make a weak syrup out of sap from the maple or the birch. Dip the leaves in the solution and eat.

As a Salad: Cut the cleaned leaves into small pieces and mix with other fresh vegetables. Pour a solution of birch sap or maple sugar sap over the greens and eat raw.

HOME RECIPES

PLANTAIN IN WHITE WINE

8 tablespoons butter	1 cup dry white wine
3 pounds plantain leaves, coarsely chopped	1 teaspoon salt
	1 teaspoon pepper
1 teaspoon wild mustard seed	2 tablespoons flour

Put a heavy 10-inch skillet over moderate heat and melt the butter. Add the plantain leaves and with two forks toss them in the melted butter until all the leaves are well coated. Slightly bruise the wild mustard seeds and add to the pan. Stir occasionally until cooked (not longer than 15 minutes). Add the wine, salt and pepper.

Bring the mixture to a boil, cover tightly and reduce the heat to a simmer. Cook for 10 minutes or until the leaves are tender.

Remove the greens from the skillet to a heated plate, leaving as much juice in the skillet as possible. Add the flour and stir with a wire whisk until the sauce is smooth and creamy. Pour over the greens and serve at once.

PLANTAIN CUSTARD RING

5 cups finely shredded young plantain leaves	1 teaspoon salt
	¼ teaspoon pepper
3 cups milk	¼ teaspoon nutmeg
6 slices bacon	1 cup dry bread crumbs
3 eggs	

Preheat oven to 375°. Clean and wash the plantain leaves under running water. Shred in fork-sized pieces. In the top of a double boiler, scald the milk and set aside. Put a 10-inch heavy skillet on high heat for 1 minute. Add the bacon slices and fry them crisp. With a slotted spoon remove the bacon and drain on paper. Crumble it with your fingers.

In a large mixing bowl, beat the eggs with an electric beater until light and fluffy. Add salt and pepper, the nutmeg and the scalded milk. Add the shredded plantain leaves, the crumbled bacon and the bacon fat together with the bread crumbs. Stir with two forks so all the leaves are well coated and the mixture is well blended.

Butter a 2-quart ring mold, making sure the ring is well greased. Add the mixture, flattening it with a spoon. Place the mold in a pan with hot water. Put the water bath with the mold in the oven to bake for 50 minutes.

Cool to room temperature and unmold on a large platter. Fill the centre with creamed peas or creamed eggs.

PLANTAIN HOT DISH

1 pound plantain leaves	1 pound ground beef
2 tablespoons butter	1 can tomato soup
3 wild onions, finely chopped	Potato chips

Preheat oven to 350°. Clean and rinse the plantain leaves under running water. Discard all brown or bruised leaves. Put a 10-inch skillet over high heat and add the butter. When the butter has a nutty smell, add the onions and brown slightly. Turn the heat down to medium and add the ground beef. Brown slightly with the onion.

Line a 3-quart greased casserole with plantain leaves. Add a layer of the meat, another layer of plantain leaves and then more meat. Continue until all the ingredients are used. Finish with a layer of plantain leaves. Pour the tomato soup over the greens and if you wish, sprinkle with crushed potato chips. Bake for 2 hours.

FRESH PLANTAIN LEAVES IN BRANDY BUTTER

2 pounds young plantain leaves	6 tablespoons brandy
8 tablespoons butter	½ teaspoon vanilla extract
½ cup superfine sugar	

Clean and rinse the plantain leaves under running water. Discard bruised or dark leaves. Shred in fork-sized pieces. Put a 12-inch heavy skillet on the fire and melt 4 tablespoons of butter over moderate heat.

When the foam subsides, add the plantain leaves and toss with 2 forks until all the leaves are coated. Put the lid on the skillet and cook for 10 minutes over moderate heat.

Combine 4 tablespoons of butter, the sugar, the brandy and vanilla extract in a large bowl. Beat the mixture with an electric beater until smooth. If you have to do it by hand, start creaming the butter by beating it against the sides of the bowl until it is light and fluffy. Add the sugar a tablespoon at a time and continue to beat until the mixture is light and fluffy. Then add the brandy and vanilla extract.

Remove the greens from the skillet with a slotted spoon and put on a well-heated platter, leaving as much of the liquid as possible in the skillet.

Add the mixture in the bowl to the skillet and make sure it blends well with the cooking juices. Add the greens and again toss with 2 forks until all the leaves are well coated. Remove from skillet to the platter, which has been cleaned and reheated. Serve at once. This dish complements meat.

BRAISED PHEASANT WITH PLANTAIN

2 pheasants	¼ cup vegetable oil
1 tablespoon salt	½ cup water
½ pound butter, softened	1 cup heavy cream
1 pound plantain leaves	¼ cup white wine
2 tablespoons butter	

Pluck and draw the pheasants. Wash thoroughly inside and out. Pat dry with paper towels. Rub the salt over the inside and outside of the birds. Using an electric beater, cream the butter on medium speed. With your hands, spread half the butter inside each bird.

Clean and wash the plantain leaves well and discard bruised or darkened leaves. Stuff the birds with the leaves, making sure they are well filled. Sew them up and tie the legs together so they will hold their shape while cooking.

Preheat the oven to 350°. In a 12-inch skillet heat 2 tablespoons of butter over high heat. When it gives off a nutty aroma, moderate the heat and add the oil. Stir well. Put the pheasants, one at a time, breast down in the skillet. After about 7 minutes, turn the bird on its side and cook for 7 minutes. Continue turning until both birds are browned on all sides.

Transfer the pheasants to a roasting pan which will easily hold both. Pour the water into the skillet and bring to a boil, stirring to get all the browned bits from the bottom. Pour the contents of the skillet over the birds, which have been placed in the roasting pan breast up. Cover tightly and braise in the middle of the oven for 1½ hours.

Remove the pheasants to a carving board and let rest for 5 minutes. Skim and discard the fat from the roasting pan juices. Add the cream and bring to a boil, stirring constantly and scraping up any browned bits from the bottom of the pan. Boil the sauce briskly for several minutes and add the wine.

Let the cream and the wine reduce and the sauce thicken. Season to taste and serve in a gravy boat.

BRAISED PLANTAIN IN RED WINE WITH HAZELNUTS

¼ pound lean bacon, diced	1½ cups beef stock
½ cup wild onion, finely chopped	1 teaspoon salt
12 cups plantain leaves, cut in strips	½ teaspoon pepper
	2 tablespoons sugar
1½ cups red wine	½ pound hazelnuts, finely chopped
2 tablespoons wine vinegar	

Preheat the oven to 350°. In a heavy 12-inch skillet cook bacon until crisp and golden. With a slotted spoon remove bacon and save. Cook the onion in the fat until it is soft but not brown.

Stir in the plantain leaves and toss with forks until all the leaves are well covered with fat.

Put the greens into a 4 to 5-quart flameproof casserole with a tight-fitting lid, and cook over low heat for 15 minutes.

Add the wine, vinegar, beef stock, salt and pepper, sugar and the bacon. Cover and bake in oven for 1 hour. Add the chopped hazelnuts, cover and put back in the oven for another hour. Make sure the liquid does not cook away too fast.

The greens are cooked when they are tender and the liquid has been absorbed.

Adjust seasoning to taste and serve from casserole.

ROLLED MOOSE FLANK STEAK STUFFED WITH PLANTAIN

2 flank steaks of moose (about 2 pounds)	4 hard-cooked eggs, cut length-wise
1 teaspoon minced wild onion	3 wild onions
1 tablespoon coarse salt	¼ cup chopped parsley
1 cup dry red wine	4 cups beef stock
1 cup water	½ cup white wine
½ pound fresh plantain leaves	3 to 4 cups water
8 Jerusalem artichoke roots, 4 inches long	2 bay leaves
	1 tablespoon salt
	3 tablespoons flour

With a sharp knife, slit the steaks horizontally along one side to within ½ inch of the other side. Open the steaks and pound them with a meat mallet to flatten them further. Trim away all gristle. Moose has very little fat.

Lay one steak in the bottom of a roaster. Scatter on half the finely chopped wild onion and coarse salt. Cover the meat with the other steak. Sprinkle it with the remaining wild onion and salt. Add the wine and water. Cover the pan and let stand for 24 hours in a cold place to marinate.

Preheat the oven to 400°. Place the steaks on a chopping board end to end, letting them overlap each other about 2 inches. Using the meat mallet, pound the steaks together to seal them securely.

Wash the plantain leaves under running water and squeeze dry. Discard all discolored or bruised leaves. Cut the Jerusalem artichoke roots into cylinders ¾ of an inch in diameter.

Spread the plantain leaves evenly over the steaks and arrange the Jerusalem artichoke cylinders across the meat in rows 3 inches apart. Place the eggs between the rows of artichokes. Slice the onions ¼ inch thick and separate into rings. Spread the rings over the eggs and artichokes and sprinkle them evenly with parsley. Carefully roll the steaks with the grain (jelly roll fashion) into a thick cylinder. Tie the roll with several rounds of kitchen string about 1 inch apart. Place it in a roasting pan and pour the beef stock over. Add the white wine and enough water to bring the liquid about ¼ up the side of the roll. Add the bay leaves and salt.

Cover the roasting pan tightly and place in the middle of the oven for 1½ to 2 hours. Remove from the oven and let rest on a heated steak platter. Add the flour and stir constantly with a wire whisk, making sure the gravy is smooth and creamy before removing from the roasting pan. With a sharp knife remove the string around the roll and place it on a carving board.

Slice crosswise in ¼-inch slices. Pour the gravy into a gravy boat and serve hot.

The roll can also be served chilled and pressed. Take it from the roasting pan as hot as possible, and place it on a chopping board. Place another board on top and weigh it down with a few heavy tins or stones. Let stand overnight in a cool place. Next day remove the weights and the top board. The pressed roll should be sliced very thinly and served on hot garlic bread.

To preserve the roll, submerge it in a weak salt brine and keep it refrigerated. The roll improves in taste the longer it stays in the brine.

DANDELION

DANDELION

(Taraxacum officinale)

The dandelion, a common pest in anyone's garden, is well-known, but a short description is in order. The flower is a composite and a beautiful golden yellow. The leaves are dark green, deeply incised and spread in a rosette at the bottom. The flowers mature into white fluffy balls which hold the seed.

The plant gets its name from the likeness of the leaves to a lion's tooth.

The tender young leaves that spring up in the spring are one of the first wild edibles to appear in Mother Nature's pantry. The young leaves are excellent in a salad or eaten raw. Later in the season they take on a bitter taste and it is preferable to cook them in two lots of water. Changing water takes away all the bitterness and makes them less tough.

Dandelions are common fare for many people and are well known for their high content of vitamin A. These plants contain twenty-five times more vitamin A than tomato juice and fifty times more than asparagus.

IN THE BUSH

As a Fresh Vegetable: The young dandelion leaves offer a delicate taste to any salad. The way I like them is in a tossed salad, slightly moistened with a syrup of sugar maple sap boiled down to half its volume, and sprinkled with finely chopped wild leeks.

As a Cooked Vegetable: Later in the season, I pluck the mature leaves and parboil them before adding them to a stew of wild game.

As Tea: For a strong tea, simmer the leaves for about ten minutes. This tea is good for colds.

As Coffee: The roots of the plant may be dried at the fireside. When they are shriveled, break them in pieces, grind between 2 stones, and use as ordinary coffee. I find 1 level teaspoon per cup is plenty.

HOME RECIPES

DANDELION SOUP WITH FRICADELLES

3 pounds beef bones	1 cup milk
5 - 6 mint leaves	2 pounds lean veal, minced
3 bay leaves	2 eggs
6 whole peppercorns	½ teaspoon salt
1 teaspoon salt	¼ teaspoon pepper
5 - 6 whole cloves	½ cup finely chopped onion
2 pounds dandelion leaves	½ cup flour
2 cups bread crumbs	½ pound butter

Put the beef bones in a 5 to 6-quart soup kettle, add 3 quarts of water and mint leaves, bay leaves, peppercorns, salt and cloves. Bring to a boil and simmer for 3 hours. Occasionally skim off the suds, being careful not to take any of the spices while skimming.

Chop the dandelion leaves coarsely and put into a 4-quart saucepan in about 2 quarts of water. Bring to a boil then simmer for 20 minutes. Remove from the heat, drain through a sieve, and set aside.

In a mixing bowl soak the bread crumbs in the milk. When thoroughly soaked add the minced veal and the eggs. Before stirring, add the salt, pepper and chopped onions, and mix well. On a piece of waxed paper, spread 1 cup of flour. Form meatballs about ½ inch in diameter, and roll in the flour.

Melt ¼ pound of butter in a skillet over high heat until it gives off a nutty aroma. Put the meatballs into the hot butter a few at a time so they can roll freely, and brown them on all sides. Remove with a slotted spoon and set aside. When all the meatballs are browned, add the rest of the butter and heat it as before. Add the dandelion leaves to the pan and stir them consantly with a fork without breaking the leaves too much. Let them sauté for 5 to 10 minutes in the butter and remove from heat.

When it is cooked, strain the beef soup through a sieve into a large bowl and wash the kettle thoroughly. Put the soup back into the clean kettle and add the dandelion leaves and fricadelles.

Let the soup simmer for at least an hour before serving as hot as possible.

FRIED SPICED DANDELION LEAVES

1 pound small spring dandelion leaves	1 tablespoon soy sauce
2 tablespoons sugar	1 teaspoon salt
2 tablespoons white vinegar	¼ teaspoon cayenne pepper
	1 tablespoon peanut oil

Cut the tender fresh dandelion leaves into 1 by 1½ inch pieces and wash well to remove all sand and grit from the leaves.

In a small bowl mix the sugar, vinegar, soy sauce, salt and cayenne pepper together and add the oil a little at a time, making sure it dissolves completely. Add the dandelion leaves and marinate for about half an hour.

Place a 10-inch skillet over high heat for about a minute. Pour in the oil, swirl around in the pan and heat for another minute, then turn the heat down to medium. Remove the dandelion leaves from the marinade with a slotted spoon and put into the hot oil. Stir for 2 to 3 minutes, making sure all the dandelion leaves are well coated with oil.

Remove the pan from the heat and stir in the marinade, mix well, and then serve on a hot platter immediately. This dish can also be served cold.

DANDELION LEAVES WITH TOASTED SESAME SEEDS

1½ pounds fresh young dandelion leaves	½ cup chicken stock
	½ teaspoon sugar
1 tablespoon salt	1 teaspoon dry mustard
1 tablespoon black sesame seeds	1 teaspoon soy sauce

Clean and wash the dandelion leaves carefully under cold running water.

In a 3-quart saucepan bring 3 cups of water to a boil and add salt. Put the dandelion leaves in the boiling water, cover tightly and cook for 5 minutes over high heat until the leaves start to wilt.

Drain the leaves and put them into cold water. This procedure stops them cooking, and you will find that the leaves will retain their fresh green color. Squeeze the leaves as dry as possible, then cut into 1-inch pieces and dry with a paper towel. Set aside.

In a heavy skillet that has been preheated over high heat for 2 minutes, toast the sesame seeds over moderate heat for 5 to 6 minutes. Shake the pan constantly until the seeds are lightly toasted.

In a small bowl mix the chicken stock, sugar, the dry mustard and the soy sauce, and stir well. Put a small saucepan on moderate heat, add the chicken stock mixture and bring to a boil over high heat. Remove from the heat and cool.

Pour the sauce over the dandelion leaves and toss together to coat the leaves thoroughly.

Divide the leaves into six small serving bowls and sprinkle the top of each with toasted sesame seeds.

CREAMED DANDELION LEAVES, CHINESE STYLE

1 pound dandelion leaves	Pepper
2 tablespoons cornstarch	½ teaspoon sugar
¼ cup milk	¾ cup chicken stock
2 tablespoons chicken fat	1 slice smoked ham ¼ inch thick,
1 teaspoon salt	finely chopped

Clean and rinse the dandelion leaves under cold running water. Cut cross-wise in 1 to 1½-inch slices. Combine the cornstarch and milk in a small bowl and stir until the cornstarch is dissolved.

Put a 10-inch skillet over high heat for a minute. Add the chicken fat, making sure it is melted and covering the bottom of the pan. Turn the heat down to medium. Add the dandelion leaves and stir until they are covered with fat. Sprinkle salt and pepper over the dish and pour in the chicken stock.

Bring the stock to a boil and cover the pan. Turn the heat to simmer for 15 minutes or until the leaves are tender. With a slotted spoon transfer the dandelion leaves to a heated platter. Bring the stock back to a boil and after stirring the cornstarch quickly to mix it well again, add it to the stock in the pan. Stir until the sauce thickens.

Pour over the dandelion leaves, sprinkle the chopped ham over the dish, and serve at once.

BRAISED DANDELION LEAVES

2 pounds fresh young dandelion leaves	1 cup beef stock
2 tablespoons butter	6 parsley sprigs
½ cup thinly sliced onion	1 bay leaf
½ cup thinly sliced carrots	2 tablespoons soft butter
8 bacon slices	3 tablespoons flour
4-inch square of bacon rind	Salt and pepper
	2 tablespoons fresh parsley

Clean the dandelion leaves well and discard any brown parts. Wash under cold running water to remove all traces of sand.

Bring 4 quarts of water and 3 tablespoons of salt to a boil in a large soup kettle. Drop the dandelion leaves into the boiling water for 10 minutes. Lift out the leaves, plunge into cold water, then drain on paper towels and sprinkle with salt and pepper.

Preheat the oven to 350°. In a 12-inch casserole with cover, melt 2 tablespoons of butter over moderate heat. When the foam subsides, put the carrots and onions in the casserole and cook them for 5 minutes, stirring constantly. Remove from heat and arrange the dandelion leaves on top of the carrots and onions and drape the bacon and the rind on top. Add the beef stock, parsley sprigs and bay leaf. Bring to a simmer on top of the stove, cover the casserole tightly, and bake on lower shelf in the oven for 1½ hours.

When serving, arrange the dandelion leaves attractively on a heated platter with the bacon slices around them. Discard bacon rind and bay leaf.

Leave 1 cup of the cooking fluid in the casserole and stir in the soft butter. When the butter has melted, add flour, salt and pepper and stir to a thin roux. Strain the sauce over the dandelion leaves and sprinkle with finely chopped parsley.

DANDELION GREENS WITH CRABAPPLE

2 pounds dandelion greens	1 cup minced wild onion
⅔ cup red wine vinegar	5 cups boiling water
2 tablespoons sugar	1 cup beef stock
2 teaspoons salt	5 tablespoons dry red wine
2 tablespoons bacon fat	3 tablespoons cranberry jelly
8 crabapples	

This recipe is particularly designed for using the dandelion leaves in late summer or early fall when they have a bitter taste.

Wash the dandelion leaves under cold running water and remove all dark or bruised parts. Shred them by slicing crosswise in ¼-inch wide strips.

Drop the leaves into a 4 to 5-quart saucepan containing 3 cups of water and 1 teaspoon salt, bring to a boil and simmer for 10 minutes. Drain the leaves thoroughly, squeezing all the water out.

Cool to room temperature. Drop greens into a large mixing bowl, sprinkle with the vinegar, sugar and salt. Toss so all the leaves are well coated.

In a heavy 4 to 5-quart casserole, melt the bacon fat over moderate heat. Peel and core crabapples and cut them into ¼-inch wedges. Cook the onion and apples in the casserole until they are lightly browned. Add the coated dandelion greens, 2 cups boiling water and the beef stock. Bring to a boil, stirring occasionally, and reduce heat. Cover the casserole and simmer for 1½ hours. Check from time to time to make sure the leaves are moist. If they seem dry, add a tablespoon of boiling water.

When they are done there should be very little liquid left. Just before serving stir in the wine and the cranberry jelly.

Can be served from the casserole or a heated platter.

DANDELION WINE

1 gallon water	4 oranges
2 quarts dandelion heads	1 teaspoon yeast nutrient
3 pounds white sugar	1 package wine yeast

This recipe makes a pleasant dandelion wine. It is important that the flowers be picked in sunshine at midday when they are fully opened and that the making of the wine should be started immediately.

In a very large kettle, bring water to a boil. Measure the yellow heads, discarding as much green as possible without being too fussy. Put flowers in a large plastic container that has been thoroughly cleaned and pour the boiling water over. Cover and leave to steep for two days. Be careful not to exceed this time or a curious odor often sets in and spoils a pleasant table wine.

Pour the water and flowers back into the kettle, add rind from the 4 oranges (no white pith) and boil for 10 minutes. Strain through a fine sieve lined with very fine cheesecloth, add the sugar and stir until it dissolves. When cool add the yeast nutrient, juice of the 4 oranges and yeast.

Put into fermentation jar and fit trap. Your fermentation jar can be a gallon jug, glass or plastic, but you must be sure it is cleaned thoroughly in hot water before use.

The fermentation trap can be obtained from any store that sells wine-making materials.

When the wine has cleared, siphon off into clean bottles with a plastic hose. Make sure the hose does not pick up any deposit on the bottom. To avoid this, attach the hose to a stick longer than the jar is tall, so that 3 inches of the stick protrude past the end of the hose and it sits on the bottom to raise the hose clear of all sediment.

This wine will be just right to serve with your Christmas poultry.

PINEAPPLE PICKLED DANDELION LEAVES

2 pounds fresh young dandelion
  leaves
6 tablespoons coarse salt
1 quart malt vinegar
¼ cup sugar
2 tablespoons mixed pickling
  spice

1 teaspoon black peppercorns
5 cups unsweetened pineapple
  juice
1 2-pound ripe pineapple

Wash the dandelion leaves under cold running water, remove all bruised or dark parts. Shred the leaves in ¼-inch strips crosswise. In a large stainless steel or enamel bowl or pot, arrange the dandelion leaves in layers and sprinkle each layer with the coarse salt. Let stand for at least 3 days in a cool place, turning them from bottom to top at least twice a day.

On the fourth day, combine vinegar, sugar, spice and pepper in a 3-quart saucepan and bring to a boil over high heat, stirring until the sugar dissolves. Boil for 8 to 10 minutes, then remove the pan from the heat.

Meanwhile, drain the dandelion leaves in a large colander. Squeeze out as much water as possible, a handful at a time, and return to the bowl. Strain the hot vinegar mixture over the leaves, turning them with a wooden spoon so all are thoroughly moist.

Cover and put in a very cool place for at least 4 to 5 days before using. Covered tightly and kept very cool, this will keep for about 3 weeks.

Take 2 pounds of the marinated dandelion leaves and wash thoroughly under cold water. Squeeze them, a handful at a time, until they are completely dry.

Combine the marinated leaves and the pineapple juice in a heavy 3 to 4-quart saucepan, and bring to a boil, stirring with a wooden spoon to separate the dandelion leaves. Reduce the heat and simmer undisturbed for 1½ to 2 hours or until the dandelion leaves have absorbed most of the cooking liquid.

With a sharp knife cut the top 2 inches off the pineapple and set the top aside. Hollow out the pineapple carefully, leaving a ¼-inch layer of fruit in the shell. With a sharp knife cut out the woody core and discard. Cut the fruit into ½-inch cubes.

Stir the diced pineapple into the cooked dandelion leaves and cook for 3 minutes, then pour the mixture into a sieve placed over a large serving bowl. When all the liquid has drained off, fill the empty pineapple shell. Put the top on and serve on a large plate, surrounded by the remaining dandelion leaves.

This dish is a wonderful complement to roast or smoked pork or game birds.

DANDELION SALAD WITH SOUR CREAM DRESSING

½ pound freshly picked young
  dandelion leaves
5 young dandelion roots
1 cup sour cream

2 tablespoons lemon juice
2 teaspoons sugar
1 teaspoon salt
½ teaspoon pepper

Clean the young dandelion greens under running water, making sure all the sand and grit is washed away. Shred to fork-sized pieces. Scrub the roots, scrape well and slice in ¼-inch rounds.

Add roots to greens and set aside in refrigerator to chill. The greens will not be taken out of the refrigerator until the last moment before serving.

Pour the sour cream into a mixing bowl. With a wooden spoon, stir in the lemon juice, sugar, salt and pepper. Beat with the wooden spoon until the sauce is smooth and creamy.

Just before serving, bring the greens out of the refrigerator and add just enough sauce to moisten the greens but not make them soggy.

Serve at once.

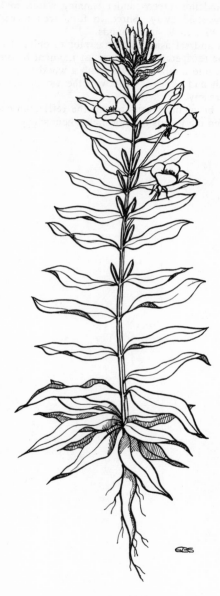

EVENING PRIMROSE

EVENING PRIMROSE

(Oenothera biennis)

The flowers of this plant are four petaled, delicate and of a yellow color. They are usually found growing from a single tall stem. The leaves are dark green and grow in a rosette around the base of the stem.

The evening primrose is familiar to most people because of the way the flowers open at dusk. The odor and the light-colored flowers attract the night-flying moths upon which they depend for fertilization. The sweet and nutritious roots caused the primrose to be one of the earliest edible plants transplanted to Europe as a food, long before the Pilgrims came to America.

The big branching roots are good only the first year. They can be eaten after this time, but they become bitter and require two water boilings. The first year plants can easily be identified because the stems with the flower spike do not appear before the second year. The leaves can be eaten raw after they have been peeled. The roots are excellent in stews or cooked by themselves.

IN THE BUSH

As a Fresh Vegetable: Take the first year's leaves and peel off the skin. Eat raw with a little salt if desired.

As a Cooked Vegetable: The way I like them best is in a stew, using the root. If I have a rabbit, I usually take the saddle (the thick back of the rump of the rabbit), cut it up in small pieces and place the meat on aluminum foil. Then I clean and scrape the roots and split them four ways as I would a carrot. I place the roots on the meat and if I have a piece of bacon or porcupine fat, I add that to the mixture. After closing up the aluminum foil tightly, I place the whole thing in the coals of my fire and let it cook for a couple of hours.

HOME RECIPES

EVENING PRIMROSE ROOT WITH HAM AND CHEESE

8 large firm primrose roots	8 thin slices smoked ham, each
1 cup cold water	about 4 by 6 inches
1 cup milk	8 slices Emmenthaler cheese, cut
1 teaspoon salt	4 by 6 inches and ⅛ inch thick

Wash the primrose roots, and scrape them. It is important to scrape them well, otherwise they will have a bitter taste. Put the roots into a 3 to 4-quart saucepan. Add a quart of water and a teaspoon of salt. Bring to a boil, turn the heat down and simmer uncovered for 10 minutes. Remove the roots with a slotted spoon and cool to room temperature.

In a 2 to 3-quart saucepan, arrange the roots in a layer and add the water, milk and salt. Bring to a boil, cover and simmer for 20 minutes or until the roots are tender but not falling apart. Preheat the oven to 375°. Remove the primrose roots from the pan with a slotted spoon and let them drain on a double thickness of paper towel. Wrap each root in a slice of ham, then in a slice of cheese.

Generously butter a shallow 8 by 10-inch flameproof casserole and arrange the wrapped roots side by side. Bake undisturbed in the middle of the oven for 15 minutes or until the cheese has melted. Serve at once directly from the casserole.

CREAM OF EVENING PRIMROSE SOUP

2 pounds evening primrose roots
2 tablespoons chopped evening
primrose leaves
6 cups chicken stock
1 teaspoon salt
7 tablespoons butter
6 tablespoons flour

2 egg yolks
½ cup cream
2 tablespoons soft butter
1 teaspoon salt
½ teaspoon pepper
Primrose leaves for garnish

Wash and clean the evening primrose roots. Peel paper thin with a sharp knife. Cut the roots into quarters lengthwise and chop them up in ½-inch pieces. Set aside. Peel the young leaves of the evening primrose and chop them finely. In a 3 to 4-quart saucepan, bring the chicken stock and the salt to a boil. Drop the primrose roots into the stock and boil for 10 to 12 minutes.

Drain the stock into a bowl and set the roots aside.

In the same saucepan, melt 5 tablespoons butter over moderate heat. Stir in the flour and beat with a wire whisk until the mixture is smooth and creamy. Remove the pan from the heat, cool for 5 minutes, and then add the stock, beating constantly. Return the pan to moderate heat and let the soup base come to a boil. Turn the heat down and simmer.

Melt the remaining butter in a 10 to 12-inch skillet over high heat and when it gives off a nutty odor, reduce the heat and add the boiled evening primrose roots to the skillet. Turn them in the butter and cook for 5 minutes.

Stir in the finely chopped leaves and cook for another 5 minutes. Stir the evening primrose roots and leaves into the simmering soup base and cook over low heat for 15 minutes, stirring from time to time.

Purée the soup through a food mill into a mixing bowl, and through a coarse sieve back into the pan. Beat the egg yolks and cream together in a small bowl .

Whisk in the puréed soup, spoonful by spoonful, until you have about 1 cup of soup mixed with the eggs and cream. Slowly add this mixture to the soup. Boil for ½ minute, stirring constantly. Remove the pan from the heat and stir in 2 tablespoons soft butter. Season with salt and pepper and add some finely chopped and peeled evening primrose leaves for color. Serve this soup from a tureen, with small pieces of evening primrose roots floating on the surface.

SCALLOPED EVENING PRIMROSE ROOTS WITH CHEESE

1 garlic clove, peeled and bruised	6 tablespoons butter
2½ pounds young evening prim- rose roots, scraped, peeled and cut into ⅛-inch slices	1 teaspoon salt
	¼ teaspoon pepper
	1¼ cups heavy cream
1½ cups grated Swiss cheese	

Preheat oven to 450°. Rub the bottom and sides of a flameproof casserole, 12 inches across and about 2 inches deep, with the bruised garlic, and grease lightly with butter. Spread half of the slices of evening primrose roots in the bottom of the dish. Sprinkle them with half the cheese. Add half the butter cut into ¼-inch squares, and salt and pepper. Cover the cheese and butter with the rest of the evening primrose roots, and place the rest of the butter, salt and pepper on top of the dish. Heat the cream on low heat and pour over top. Bring to a simmer on top of the stove. Bake in the oven for 30 minutes or until the evening primrose roots are tender. Remove excess fluid with a bulb baster and replace the casserole in the oven for another 5 minutes to brown the top of the dish. Serve hot.

FISH PICKLED WITH EVENING PRIMROSE AND ONION

6 tablespoons butter	2 large bay leaves, crumbled
2 pounds pickerel or lake trout fillets, cut about ¾ inch thick	2 teaspoons finely chopped garlic
	2 teaspoons salt
6 wild onions, cut in rings	¼ teaspoon cayenne pepper
5 medium-sized evening primrose roots, scraped and peeled	¼ teaspoon white pepper
	1 cup dry white wine
1 cup dry white wine	

In a heavy 12-inch skillet, melt 2 tablespoons of butter over high heat. When the butter gives off a nutty smell, lower the heat and add the fish fillets. Cook them for 3 minutes on each side, turning them with a large fish spatula.

When golden brown remove from the skillet and dry on paper towels.

Clean the skillet and melt the rest of the butter over high heat. When the butter gives off a nutty odor, lower the heat and add the onion rings. Cook for 8 minutes or until the onion rings are golden brown. Stir in the evening primrose roots, wine, bay leaves, garlic, salt and the red and white pepper. Simmer for 15 minutes or until the evening primrose roots are tender. Remove roots from the skillet with a slotted spoon and set aside. Add another cup of wine and simmer for 5 minutes more.

Take a quart sealer, place half of the fish on the bottom of the sealer and pour half of the marinade from the skillet over the fish. Add a layer of evening primrose roots on top, then another layer of fish and another layer of roots. Pour in the rest of the marinade from the skillet. Cover tightly with the lid from the sealer and refrigerate for at least 4 days before serving.

If you wish to add some color, scrape and clean 1 carrot, cut crosswise in ¼-inch slices and add to the sealer. Serve this dish from the sealer.

EVENING PRIMROSE ROOT AND ONION OMELET WITH PEPPERONI

1½ cups vegetable oil	1 4-ounce package pepperoni
2 pounds young evening primrose roots	4 eggs
	2 teaspoons salt
½ cup wild onion, minced	

Peel the evening primrose roots and slice in ¼-inch rounds. In a heavy 12-inch skillet, heat the vegetable oil over high heat until a light haze forms over the skillet. Add the roots. Sprinkle them with the salt and turn them over until they are well coated on all sides.

Reduce the heat to moderate and cook for 15 minutes. Slice the pepperoni crosswise in ¼-inch rounds. Add the chopped onion and pepperoni to the skillet. Cook, stirring occasionally, for another 10 minutes.

Transfer the entire contents of the skillet to a large sieve or colander and drain off the excess oil. Preheat the oven to 425°.

Break the eggs into a large bowl and add the salt. Beat with an electric beater until the eggs are frothy. Grease a 2-quart casserole on the bottom and sides thoroughly, and add the egg mixture. Gently stir in the primrose roots, onions and pepperoni. Place the casserole in the middle of the oven and bake for 30 minutes or until a knife inserted in the middle comes out dry. It may be necessary to cover the casserole with a piece of aluminum foil to prevent the top from burning.

EVENING PRIMROSE ROOT BALLS

1 cup bread crumbs	½ pound finely minced smoked ham
½ cup milk	
1 tablespoon dry mustard	1 egg, lightly beaten
4 medium-sized primrose roots, boiled and minced	1 teaspoon salt
	½ teaspoon pepper
1 pound lean fresh pork, finely minced	2 tablespoons butter
	2 tablespoons vegetable oil
	1 cup dry red wine

Soak the bread crumbs in the milk until they are completely soggy. Mix the dry mustard with a tablespoon of red wine, making sure the mustard is smooth.

Combine the minced primrose roots, the minced pork, and the minced smoked ham in a large mixing bowl. Add the bread crumbs, mustard, the lightly beaten egg, salt and pepper and mix them thoroughly together. Form the mixture into small balls about 1 inch in diameter and chill for ¾ of an hour.

Preheat the oven to 350°. Over high heat, melt the butter and the oil in a large heavy skillet. When the foam subsides, add the meatballs a few at a time. To keep the balls in shape, roll them around in the fat by shaking the skillet back and forth over the burner. When the meatballs are well browned on all sides, remove them from the skillet with a slotted spoon and put them into a 2-quart casserole. Pour off all but a thin film of fat from the skillet and pour in the wine. Bring to a boil, scraping up any brown bits from the root balls.

Pour the wine into the casserole. Cover tightly and bake in the middle of the oven for about 30 minutes, basting the root balls from time to time.

Serve directly from the casserole, or place the root balls and sauce in a chafing dish and serve, speared with tooth picks, as an accompaniment to cocktails or a midnight snack.

EVENING PRIMROSE ROOT SOUP

2 cups evening primrose roots
2½ cups Jerusalem artichoke roots
Juice of 2 lemons
2 tablespoons butter
1 pound boneless beef chuck, cut into 1-inch cubes
2 quarts water
1 pound beef marrow bones, sawed into 1-inch pieces

1 large onion, pierced with 2 whole cloves
2 bay leaves
1 teaspoon salt
½ teaspoon pepper
1 cup coarsely diced leeks or wild onion
1 tablespoon chopped parsley
Dumplings

Clean and scrape the primrose roots well and dice coarsely. Clean and scrape the skin of the Jerusalem artichoke well, removing all black spots. Dice coarsely and put both the evening primrose roots and the Jerusalem artichoke roots in a pot with water to which the lemon juice has been added. This is to prevent the roots from blackening.

In a 5 to 6-quart soup pot, melt the butter over high heat and when it gives off a nutty odor, add the beef. Stir with a wooden spoon, making sure all the beef gets nicely browned. Add the water and the bones and boil over high heat, skimming off the foam as it rises to the surface. Reduce the heat to a gentle simmer. Add the onion with the cloves, bay leaves, salt and pepper. Simmer partly covered for 1½ hours, skimming whenever necessary. While the soup boils make the dumplings.

DUMPLINGS

3 cups all purpose flour
1 teaspoon salt
¼ teaspoon nutmeg

4 eggs
1 cup milk
¼ pound butter

In a large mixing bowl, combine the flour, ½ teaspoon salt and the nutmeg. Break the eggs over the flour and beat them in. Pour in the milk a little at a time, stirring with a large wooden spoon until the dough is smooth.

Bring 2 quarts of water and ½ teaspoon of salt to a boil in a 4 to 5-quart saucepan. With a tablespoon, form small balls of the dough and drop into the boiling water, making sure each forms firmly before the next ball is put into the water. When all the dough is used up, boil for 8 to 10 minutes. Then drain off the water or remove the dumplings with a slotted spoon and set aside.

Remove the onion and the bay leaves from the soup pot and discard them. Transfer the bones to a plate. With a small knife remove the marrow and add to the soup.

Add the drained evening primrose roots, leeks and Jerusalem artichoke roots to the soup and simmer for an hour or until the roots are tender. Add the dumplings and simmer for 4 to 5 minutes to heat them thoroughly.

Add the parsley. Check for seasoning and serve from a heated soup tureen.

GREAT BURDOCK

GREAT BURDOCK

(Arctium lappa)

The heads of great burdock are long stalked, often in groups of three. The large leaves are shaped like oblong hearts and are rough and purplish, with veins. The sticky burrs which attach themselves easily to man are a familiar nuisance. Some varieties of burdock are cultivated and highly prized in Japan and elsewhere in the Eastern Hemisphere.

The plant came to America with the early settlers and has since spread all over the continent.

The burdock is a topnotch survival food because it is easily recognized and cannot be mistaken for anything else. No one has to stay hungry where this versatile plant grows because it can be converted into several different delicacies. In gathering it for food it is wise to look for the first year's roots, which are milder in taste. The first year's plant is easily distinguished, as the biennials stemming from it have no flowers or burrs.

IN THE BUSH

The tender roots are prepared in the same way as you would peel parsnips. Sliced, they make an extremely good potherb.

If picked early enough, the young leaves can be boiled and served as greens. The rapidly growing flower stalk is the tastiest part of the burdock. Every shred of the bitter skin has to be removed by peeling.

The pith of the flower stalks has long been used for candy.

As a Cooked Vegetable: Dig up the root, peel and slice. Put into boiling water and let boil for 20 minutes. Drain off the first water. Then barely cover the roots with water again and add a pinch of salt if you have it. Add the carcasses of birds or squirrels.

As a Fresh Vegetable: The peeled young leaf stalks are good eaten raw or in a salad. I like them best peeled, cut in pieces and marinated in birch sap for a couple of days.

41

HOME RECIPES

BURDOCK AND CRAWFISH HOT DISH

½ cup canning salt
12 medium-sized crawfish (or shrimp)
1 bunch dill
1 teaspoon salt
1 cup wild rice (or domestic)

1 10-ounce can mushrooms and juice
1 can cream of chicken soup
1 can chicken with rice soup
2 tablespoons butter
1½ pounds peeled burdock stalks
½ cup cheddar cheese

Fill a 4 to 5-quart pan with water. Bring to a furious boil and add the canning salt. Then take one crawfish at a time and put into the boiling water, making sure the water comes to a boil before the next is added. When all crawfish are in, put the dill into the pot and boil for 15 minutes. Take off the fire and let stand in a cool place until the crawfish are completely cold. Take out the crawfish and using a sharp knife, peel off the shells.

This is easily done as follows: Break off the tail and the claws and discard the body. Break open the claws by inserting the knife in the open part of the claw and using it as a can opener. Remove the white meat and put in a bowl. The tail is opened in the same way. Insert the knife in the open end and pry upwards. After you get the white meat out, remove the black strip along the back of the tail and put the meat in the bowl.

In a 3-quart saucepan, bring 2 quarts of water to a boil. Add the salt, and slowly add the wild rice without letting the boiling subside. Simmer for 30 minutes or until the rice is soft all through the kernel. Drain and set aside.

Mix the cream of chicken soup and the chicken with rice soup together with the rice. Butter a casserole and spread the rice mixture in a thin layer over the bottom. On top of this put a layer of crawfish and mushroom. Cut the burdock stalks into 3-inch lengths and place a layer over the crawfish and mushroom. Alternate the layers until all the ingredients are used. Sprinkle cheese on top and bake for 45 minutes in a 350° oven. Serve as hot as possible.

BURDOCK FISH SOUP

FISH STOCK

½ cup coarsely chopped, peeled burdock root
½ cup coarsely chopped, peeled burdock stalk
3 wild onions, peeled and quartered
1 teaspoon salt

2 large Jerusalem artichokes, peeled and chopped
2 tablespoons black mustard seeds
2 pounds of fish trimmings (heads, bones, etc.), washed
4 quarts cold water

To prepare the fish stock which will be the base of the soup, combine all the ingredients in a 4 to 5-quart soup kettle. Bring to a boil. Partly cover the pan and simmer for 40 minutes. Strain the stock through a fine sieve into a large bowl, pressing down hard on the vegetables and fish trimmings with the back of a spoon. Wash the pan and return the strained stock to it. Reduce the stock by boiling over high heat until the volume is about 6 cups. Strain again through a double cheesecloth.

SOUP

6 cups fish stock	2 egg yolks
½ cup finely chopped, peeled burdock roots	Salt
	Pepper
½ cup finely chopped, peeled burdock stalks	Freshly ground mustard seeds
	3 tablespoons chopped parsley
½ cup finely sliced leeks	6 tablespoons sour cream
1 pound boneless pickerel in 2 fillets	

Put the stock in the pot. Add the finely chopped burdock, the sliced leeks and the fish. As soon as it comes to a boil, lower the heat and simmer uncovered for about 10 minutes. Remove from heat, lift the fish out with a slotted spoon and set aside on a platter. Beat the egg yolks with a wire whisk, then beat in about 1 cup of the hot stock, 1 tablespoon at a time. Pour the mixture into the soup slowly, beating continuously with a whisk. Separate the fish into flakes and add to the soup. Season the soup with salt, pepper and mustard seeds. Do not let the soup boil at this stage. Serve in individual bowls and sprinkle with chopped parsley.

Garnish with 1 tablespoon of sour cream to each serving.

WATERCRESS AND BURDOCK SOUP

2 cups fresh watercress	½ cup wild onion, finely chopped
10 cups water	2 tablespoons flour
¼ pound lean bacon, in one piece	2 tablespoons cider vinegar
2 leeks, finely chopped	2 frankfurters, sliced into ¼-inch rounds
3 large burdock roots, scraped and cleaned	1 teaspoon salt
3 burdock stalks, finely chopped	Freshly ground pepper
2 tablespoons bacon fat	

Wash the watercress under cold running water. In a heavy 4-quart casserole, bring the water to a boil over high heat. Add the watercress, bacon, chopped leek, burdock roots and stalks. Return to a boil, reduce the heat to simmer, and cover for 30 minutes.

Melt the bacon fat over moderate heat in a heavy skillet and when it begins to splutter, add the onion. Cook for 10 minutes or until the onions are lightly colored. Sprinkle flour over them. Lower the heat and cook, stirring constantly, until the flour turns golden brown. Be careful not to burn it — regulate the heat accordingly. Ladle about ½ cup of the simmering soup into the browned flour and beat vigorously with a whisk until smooth and thick. Stir in the vinegar. With a spatula, scrape the entire contents of the skillet into the boiling watercress and stir thoroughly.

Cover the casserole and simmer over low heat for another 30 minutes.

Before serving, cut the bacon into small pieces and return to the soup with the sliced frankfurters. Simmer for 5 minutes to heat the meat thoroughly. Stir in the salt and grind in pepper generously.

BURDOCK PATTIES

4 cups peeled and sliced burdock root	1 egg, well beaten
1 teaspoon salt	¼ cup finely chopped parsley
2 tablespoons butter	½ cup bread crumbs
½ cup chopped wild onion	½ cup cornflakes
	3 tablespoons bacon dripping

Put the sliced and peeled burdock roots in a 3-quart saucepan and fill with 2 quarts water and a teaspoon of salt. Bring to a boil. Turn the heat down and simmer for 25 minutes or until the roots are soft and tender. Drain off the water and mash the drained burdock roots. Add salt. In a skillet melt the butter and add the chopped onion. Cook on high heat until the onions are brown. Set aside to cool slightly.

Mix the mashed burdock roots and the onions. Add the well-beaten egg and the chopped parsley. Stir in the bread crumbs. Form into patties about 2½ inches in diameter and 1 inch thick. Roll in cornflakes.

Melt the bacon fat in a skillet until it starts smoking. Put the patties into the fat and cook until nicely browned on both sides.

BURDOCK CASSEROLE

½ cup chopped wild onion	Salt and pepper
10 stalks of burdock shoots, peeled and cleaned	½ cup bread crumbs
3 tablespoons butter	1 tablespoon chopped parsley
1 can beef consommé	Pimento strips

Spread chopped onion in a greased casserole. On top of this arrange the burdock shoots and dot with butter. Add the consommé and bake at 400° for 30 minutes. Add salt and pepper to taste. Five minutes before the casserole is finished, take out and sprinkle with bread crumbs and put back in the oven. Garnish with parsley and pimento, and serve from the casserole.

SCALLOPED BURDOCK WITH TOMATO

5 cups sliced, peeled burdock shoots	3 teaspoons sugar
2 cups canned tomatoes	¼ teaspoon pepper
3 wild onions, chopped	4 tablespoons butter
½ teaspoon salt	2 tablespoons flour
	1 cup cracker crumbs

Peel and cut the burdock shoots in ½-inch lengths. In a 2-quart saucepan, combine the burdock, tomatoes, onions, salt, sugar and pepper. Bring the mixture to a boil. Lower the heat and simmer for 15 minutes. In a small saucepan melt the butter and stir in the flour. Make a smooth paste and stir it into the burdock mixture. Cook until thick.

Grease a casserole and pour in the mixture. Sprinkle the top with the cracker crumbs.

Bake for 15 minutes in a 400° oven or until the top is nicely browned.

BURDOCK ROOTS WITH BRAISED PORK CHOPS

6 lean pork chops	3 tablespoons peanut oil
3 tablespoons soy sauce	10 medium-sized burdock roots
2 teaspoons sugar	2 tablespoons water
4 tablespoons dry sherry	

Trim most of the fat off the pork chops. On a chopping board, pound each chop with a meat mallet on both sides. Combine 2 tablespoons of soy sauce, the sugar and 2 tablespoons of sherry. Blend well and pour over the chops.

Coat the chops with the sauce and lay them side by side on a sheet of wax paper. In a heavy 12-inch skillet, heat 2 tablespoons of oil over high heat and when it starts to smoke, reduce the heat. Add 3 pork chops and cook for 3 minutes on each side or until they are golden brown. With kitchen tongs transfer the chops to a heated plate. Add the remaining oil and brown the rest of the pork chops.

Scrape and peel the burdock roots. Wash well, and over a mixing bowl, grate in fine shreds. Add the shredded burdock roots to the remaining oil in the skillet and stir-fry for 5 minutes over high heat. Return the pork chops to the pan and sprinkle with the remaining soy sauce and sherry. Add the water and cover tightly. Reduce the heat to simmer and cook the chops and the burdock roots for 30 minutes.

To serve, transfer the pork chops to a large heated serving platter and spread the burdock on top of them.

BOILED BEEF AND BURDOCK

3 pounds lean brisket, rolled and tied	20 peeled wild onions
	20 peeled burdock stalks
1 teaspoon salt	1 teaspoon pepper
1 cup dry red wine	Dumplings

Place the brisket in a 3 to 4-quart casserole, add water to cover, the salt and the wine. Bring to a boil over high heat, skimming off the scum and foam as they rise to the surface. Reduce the heat, cover the casserole, and simmer for 2 hours.

Add the onions, burdock stalks and pepper, and cook partially covered for another 35 minutes or until the stalks are tender and the meat shows no resistance when pierced with a fork. I usually serve this dish with dumplings.

DUMPLINGS

1 cup all purpose flour	1½ to 2 tablespoons ground suet, chilled
½ teaspoon double acting baking powder	½ cup milk
½ teaspoon salt	

Sift the flour, baking powder and salt into a large mixing bowl. Add the suet and rub the fat and flour together with your fingers until it gets flaky. Pour the milk over the mixture, toss lightly and gather the dough into a ball. With lightly floured hands, shape the dough into 1-inch balls.

With a slotted spoon, remove the meat and vegetables from the stock and keep warm. If there is not enough stock left in the casserole to cook the dumplings, add more liquid made up of half beef stock and half wine.

Place the casserole over high heat and when the stock starts to bubble, lower the heat. Drop the dumplings into the hot liquid, stirring once or twice. Cook for 20 minutes over low heat or until the dumplings rise to the surface.

Place the dumplings around the meat and vegetables on a heated platter and serve at once.

BAKED BURDOCK OMELET

1 cup burdock roots	¼ teaspoon salt
4 eggs	2 tablespoons butter

Clean the burdock roots thoroughly and peel. Cut lengthwise in quarters. Put in a 2-quart saucepan and cover with water. Bring to a boil over high heat. Lower the heat and simmer for 15 minutes or until the roots are tender.

Preheat the oven to 400°. In a small bowl, beat the eggs and salt with a rotary beater until they are well combined. Set aside. Heat the butter in a 10-inch stainless steel skillet over high heat. When the butter gives off a nutty odor, reduce the heat. Drop the drained burdock roots into the skillet and cook them for 10 minutes or until they are golden brown.

Spread the burdock roots over the bottom of a 1-quart baking and serving dish and pour the eggs over them. Bake in the upper half of the oven for 20 minutes or until the omelet is firm.

LAMB'S-QUARTERS

LAMB'S-QUARTERS

(Chenopodium album)

The stems of this plant, ranging in height from one to three feet, are erect and green in color, becoming reddish towards the base. The leaves, with or without basal lobes, have margins either lobed or toothed. The flowers are green and are crowded together in small clusters.

In many homes across the continent lamb's-quarters is the only wild plant which is picked and used as a household green. The tender tops of this plant have none of the strong taste the market varieties have.

The entire young plant is delicious. Even from the older plant you can usually collect new shoots for a crisp salad. This plant does not need parboiling and in taste is very much like cabbage.

The Indians long ago used the ripe seeds (as many as 70,000 have been counted on one single plant) for cereal and for grinding into meal.

These tiny seeds, which come from elongated dense clusters, are also handy for giving a pumpernickel taste to bread and biscuits.

Lamb's-quarters is found in all parts of North America. No matter where you live in the North or South, East or West, you can usually find plenty of young plants up to about a foot tall, and that is what we are looking for.

IN THE BUSH

As a Fresh Vegetable: The leaves are very good cleaned and made into a salad, flavored with the seeds. I like it best with wild mustard seeds added and a weak solution of fermented maple sap poured over.

As a Gruel: Collect as many seeds as you can and grind them between 2 stones. Add some water and boil to a thick gruel or mush. Eat as you would porridge. If berries are in season, add some crushed berries on top of the gruel.

In Cakes: Prepare the seeds as for gruel. Form the gruel into cakes and bake slowly over the fire or in a reflector oven made out of flat stones. They taste like buckwheat and are very nutritious.

HOME RECIPES
LAMB'S-QUARTERS SOUP WITH MEATBALLS

2 pounds fresh lamb's-quarters
   leaves
2 quarts beef stock
4 slices white bread
1 cup milk
2 eggs
2 teaspoons salt

Pepper
2 pounds ground beef
3 tablespoons butter
2 tablespoons flour
½ teaspoon nutmeg
3 hard-boiled eggs

Wash the leaves thoroughly under cold running water to remove sand and grit. Drain by shaking vigorously by hand or use a lettuce basket, then chop coarsely, put in a 4-quart saucepan and add the beef stock. Bring to a boil, lower the heat and simmer.

Remove crusts from the slices of white bread and soak in the milk. When completely soggy add the eggs, salt and pepper, and mix well. Then add the minced meat and mix thoroughly.

Out of the meat mixture make small meatballs and add to the boiling soup. Simmer for at least 20 minutes.

Melt the butter in a saucepan. When the foam subsides, remove the pan from the heat and stir in the flour. With a wire whisk beat in 1 cup of stock a little at a time. When the roux is smooth and creamy, stir it into the lamb's-quarters soup. Add the nutmeg and more salt and pepper if necessary for taste.

Partly cover the pan and simmer for 20 minutes more, stirring occasionally. Garnish each serving of soup with a few slices of the hard-boiled eggs.

BRAISED LAMB'S-QUARTERS

2 pounds freshly picked lamb's-
   quarters leaves
4 tablespoons butter, cut into
   small pieces
2 tablespoons sugar

2 teaspoons salt
½ cup water
½ cup vinegar
¾ cup red currant jelly
½ cup grated apple

Wash the leaves under cold running water. Remove all bruised parts and discard. Slice very finely. You should have about 9 cups of shredded leaves when finished.

Preheat the oven to 350°. Over high heat combine the butter, sugar, salt, water and vinegar in a heavy 4 to 5-quart enameled or glass casserole. When the mixture comes to a boil and the butter has melted, add the lamb's-quarters and toss thoroughly with two wooden spoons. Bring to a boil again, cover tightly and place in the center of the oven to braise for 2 hours. Check the level of fluid occasionally and add a little vinegar if necessary.

About 10 minutes before the cooking time is finished stir in the jelly and the grated apple.

This dish will improve in taste if after it has cooled it is kept in the refrigerator for a day or so. When you are ready to use it, reheat at 325° for 1 hour.

This dish is served as a complement to ham or pork.

SWEET AND SOUR LAMB'S-QUARTERS

1½ pounds lamb's-quarters leaves	4 tablespoons vinegar
4 strips bacon	4 tablespoons brown sugar
4 tablespoons butter	2 teaspoons caraway seeds
2 wild onions, finely chopped	½ teaspoon salt
1 apple, diced	¼ teaspoon pepper
2 cups water	

Wash the lamb's-quarters leaves under running water, shred very finely and place in a 3-quart saucepan. Fry the bacon and when it is very crisp, take it out of the skillet and set aside. Pour the bacon fat over the shredded lamb's-quarters leaves and sauté for 10 minutes. Add the onions and boil for 10 minutes, constantly turning the leaves over gently without breaking them up. Add the diced apple, water, vinegar, brown sugar and the caraway seed. Simmer for about 20 minutes over medium heat, stirring gently from time to time. Add salt and pepper. At the very last add the butter, and when the butter is completely melted and absorbed by the leaves, serve hot.

LAMB'S-QUARTERS ROLLS

4 slices white bread	1 pound minced beef
1 cup milk	20 of the largest lamb's-quarters
2 eggs	leaves you can find
1 teaspoon salt	4 tablespoons butter
½ teaspoon pepper	1 cup molasses

In a large mixing bowl soak the bread (crusts removed) in the milk. When the bread is soaked through, add the eggs and the salt and pepper. Stir thoroughly. Add the minced beef and mix again.

Fill a 4-quart saucepan with 1 quart water and bring to a boil. When the water is boiling put the lamb's-quarters leaves in and cook for 10 minutes. Take off the heat and drain thoroughly. When the leaves have cooled enough to handle, take a tablespoon of meat and roll it up in a leaf. Continue, using 1 leaf to 1 tablespoon meat, until all the leaves are rolled. Grease a casserole well and place the meat-filled leaves side by side in it. Spread the butter on top of the filled leaves and pour the molasses over the whole dish. Put into the oven at 425° and bake for 2 hours. Occasionally baste the rolls with the fluid in the casserole, using a bulb baster. This dish is served hot with baked potatoes.

LAMB'S-QUARTERS KAPOSZTA STYLE

2 pounds lamb's-quarters leaves	1 teaspoon minced garlic
½ cup coarse salt	2 tablespoons paprika
½ cup brown sugar	1 pound Polish sausage cut into
1 cup vinegar	¼-inch slices
1 pound bacon, solid piece with	2 cups chicken stock
rind	¾ cup milk
1 cup wild rice	1½ cups sour cream
Salt and pepper	½ teaspoon salt
2 pounds boneless pork, cut into	Pepper
¾-inch cubes	½ teaspoon paprika
1½ cups minced wild onions	

Marinate the lamb's-quarters leaves as follows: In an earthenware crock place a layer of leaves, salt and brown sugar, another layer of leaves and more salt and sugar and so on till all the leaves are used up. Add 1 cup vinegar. Place a weight on top of the leaves such as a plate with a couple of cans on top. Let stand in a cool place for 3 to 4 days.

Preheat the oven to 350°. Wash the marinated leaves under cold running water, squeeze them dry and set aside.

With a sharp knife cut the rind off the bacon, leaving about ¼ inch of the fat still attached to the rind. Dice the bacon into ¼-inch chunks. Cook in a skillet until crisp, then transfer it to a large mixing bowl. Pour off all the fat from the skillet and save it.

Fill a 2-quart saucepan with 1 quart of water, bring it to a boil, gently immerse the wild rice and cook for 30 minutes. Pour into a strainer and stand it close to the heat so the rice can dry.

On a platter mix some salt and pepper, and roll the pork cubes in this. Heat 5 tablespoons of the bacon fat in a skillet until it starts to smoke, and toss the cubes in the skillet for 8 to 10 minutes or until they are lightly browned on all sides. With a slotted spoon transfer the pork into the mixing bowl with the bacon. Add the onions and garlic to the fat remaining in the skillet and cook for 10 minutes or until the onions are lightly brown. Take off the heat and stir in the paprika to coat the onions, then transfer the mixture into the mixing bowl with the bacon and fat.

Return the skillet to the heat, add the sausage slices and cook until they are lightly browned. Add to the mixture in the bowl. Clean the skillet over the fire with 1 cup of chicken stock, making sure you get all the brown bits which may have stuck to the bottom. Empty the contents of the skillet into the mixing bowl with a fork, stirring gently to mix all the ingredients well.

Preheat oven to 375°. Line a heavy 6-quart casserole with the leaves of the lamb's-quarters after pulling them apart with your fingers. Spread the mixture from the bowl over the leaves in an even layer, and on top of this spread the rice. Mix the milk and the sour cream and pour over the rice evenly. Now take the bacon rind, score it and cut into 5 or 6 equal strips. Place those strips over the top of the casserole and on top sprinkle the salt, a little pepper and the paprika. Heat the casserole over medium heat until it boils, then transfer into the middle of the oven. Bake for 1½ hours.

This dish is served direct from the casserole.

CREAM PORRIDGE OF LAMB'S-QUARTERS SEEDS

1½ cups flour made from lamb's-quarters seeds	1 cup scalded milk
2 tablespoons butter	4 tablespoons sugar
3 cups sour cream	1 tablespoon cinnamon

With a rolling pin, crush the lamb's-quarters seeds on a cutting board between two towels. Make sure you have a fine powder when you are finished.

In a 3-quart saucepan melt the butter over medium heat. Add the sour cream and bring to a boil. Add enough lamb's-quarters flour to make a medium thick mush, using an old-fashioned Dover beater to ensure smoothness. Stir constantly, and as butter rises to the surface pour it off and save.

Keep stirring until no more butter comes to the surface. Then add more flour to make a thick mush. Beat well and thin to desired consistency by adding scalded milk.

Serve with the melted butter and sprinkle with sugar and cinnamon. Pour cold milk over top.

ROAST GOOSE WITH LAMB'S-QUARTERS

8 to 10-pound goose	1 cup grated arrowhead tubers
1 cup water	2 tablespoons lamb's-quarters
4 pounds fresh lamb's-quarters	seeds
leaves	½ teaspoon pepper
2 cups minced wild onions	½ teaspoon salt
2 cups finely chopped apples	

Preheat the oven to 350°. Clean the goose thoroughly, removing all the fat from the inside. Chop the fat into ½-inch chunks and simmer in a small covered saucepan with the water for 15 minutes. Uncover the pan and boil off all the liquid. When the fat starts to sputter, leave on low heat and cook till the sputtering stops. Strain the fat in a sieve over a small bowl and set aside. Discard any browned fat.

Clean and wash the lamb's-quarters leaves, discarding all bruised or dark leaves. Squeeze them dry and set aside. Heat 8 tablespoons of the goose fat in a 12-inch heavy skillet over·high heat. When the fat starts to smoke lower the heat, add the wild onions and cook for 8 minutes or until the onions are transparent but not brown. Add the lamb's-quarters leaves and cook, stirring constantly, for 15 minutes.

Transfer the lamb's-quarters mixture to a large mixing bowl. Add the finely chopped apples, grate the arrowhead tubers over the bowl, and add the lamb's-quarters seeds, well crushed, the salt and the pepper.

Wash the goose with cold running water, pat it dry with paper towels and sprinkle salt and pepper inside the cavity. Stuff with the lamb's-quarters mixture and sew up the opening with a curved needle and thread.

Truss the goose and set it on a rack in the roasting pan with the breast up. Cook in the middle of the oven for 2½ hours. Using a bulb baster, baste the bird from time to time with the fat from the bottom of the roasting pan. The goose is done when the fluid emerging from a puncture is pale yellow.

Remove the bird to a serving dish and cut all the thread away. Place the stuffing all around the bird.

MILKWEED

MILKWEED

(Asclepias syriaca)

The stems of the milkweed are from 2 to 5 feet tall, unbranched, finely hairy and with a milky juice. The leaves are large, opposite one another, short stalked, oblong in shape, with prominent veins. They are green on the upper surface but light colored and velvety hairy on the lower surface.

The small, purplish, fragrant flowers are in umbellate clusters at the top of the stem. The mature seedpods are 3 to 4 inches long and covered with soft spines and hair.

Because the milkweed can be used only a short time of the year, it never became an important food for the Indians or the early settlers, and therefore it is hard to trace the history of this plant. Nevertheless, we know the Ojibway and the New England Micmac Indians considered the milkweed a delicacy, but we cannot discover how widely it was used.

IN THE BUSH

The young shoots of milkweed may be boiled in the spring. The older stems are too acid and milky for use, but the very young seed pods are excellent when cooked.

As a Cooked Vegetable: Collect the young shoots of milkweed, wash them well and cut into 2-inch pieces. I like to take the thin skin off the stalks because you get a better-tasting vegetable this way. Since they are a very delicate vegetable in the early spring, they should, to my taste, not be boiled but steamed. I usually wrap the young stalks in a large water lily leaf and put the leaf on the coals to cook for about 15 minutes.

The young seed pods, no larger than a walnut, I usually fry in fat of any kind. If I have a little flour, I mix this into the fat and make a stew of the pods.

HOME RECIPES
MILKWEED PODS SOUP

1 pound young milkweed pods	10 cups water
1 cup coarsely chopped milkweed stalks	1 cup chicken stock
1 cup coarsely chopped wild onion	1 teaspoon salt
	½ teaspoon pepper
1 pound smoked ham, diced	4 hard-cooked eggs
	2 tablespoons red wine

Wash the milkweed pods well under running water and transfer to a large soup pot. Peel the thin skin from the stalks and cut them into small pieces. Add them with the chopped onions and the ham to the pot, then pour in the water and place over high heat on the stove. Skim off the scum that rises to the surface. Cover the pot and simmer for 2 hours.

Remove the ham and purée the soup through a food mill or sieve. Return the purée and all its liquid to the soup pot and add the chicken stock until you have the right consistency. This soup should be medium thick. Taste for seasoning and add salt and pepper. Bring the soup to a simmer. Peel and chop the hard-boiled eggs into small pieces and stir into the soup together with the wine. Let stand for a few minutes to settle. Serve as hot as possible. If you wish, you can garnish with a slice of lemon with a small sprig of parsley on top.

CREAM OF MILKWEED PODS SOUP

1 pound milkweed pods	1 egg yolk
2 cups beef stock	1 cup light cream
2 cups cold water	1 teaspoon salt
4 tablespoons butter	¼ teaspoon pepper
½ cup flour	¼ teaspoon lemon juice

Clean and wash the milkweed pods under running water and cut crosswise into ¼-inch lengths. In a 2-quart heavy saucepan combine the pods, water and beef stock, bring to a boil over high heat, lower the heat and simmer for 15 minutes. Remove the milkweed pods from the pan to a large bowl and set aside. Save the stock.

Melt the butter in a 4-quart saucepan. Stir in the flour a little at a time and make a smooth roux, making sure all the lumps are dissolved. Cook for 2 to 3 minutes over a low heat, stirring constantly. Pour in the saved stock while beating steadily with a wire whisk. Increase the heat and let the mixture come to a boil. It should be somewhat thick and smooth. Simmer for 4 to 5 minutes and add the milkweed pods. Continue simmering for 15 to 20 minutes over low heat. Beat the egg yolk and cream with a fork in a small bowl. Add ½ cup of the hot purée, a little at a time. Stir the egg mixture slowly into the pot with the milkweed pods and simmer for 5 minutes, stirring constantly. Do not boil. Season with salt, pepper and lemon juice, and serve in individual soup bowls.

YOUNG MILKWEED PODS, BLANCHED AND BUTTERED

4 quarts water	4 tablespoons butter
2 tablespoons salt	1 teaspoon salt
2 pounds milkweed pods	½ teaspoon pepper

Clean and rinse the milkweed pods under running water. Put with the water and salt into a large kettle. Place on the stove over high heat and bring to a boil. Cook for 3 minutes, then remove the milkweed pods and plunge them into cold water. Leave for 2 minutes then drain in a large sieve. Melt the butter over high heat in a 3-quart saucepan. When it gives off a nutty aroma, lower the heat and add the milkweed pods, tossing them gently to make sure they are coated with butter on all sides. Add the salt and pepper and transfer to a serving dish.

This dish can be prepared ahead of time. After the milkweed pods have come out of the cold water and are thoroughly drained, place in a bowl and refrigerate. If you plan to serve them hot, melt the butter in a saucepan and add the milkweed pods to be reheated in the butter, season them to taste and serve.

MILKWEED STALKS AND WILD ONIONS IN SOUR CREAM

4 tablespoons butter	1 teaspoon lemon juice
8 wild onions	1 teaspoon salt
1 pound peeled milkweed stalks	½ teaspoon pepper
1 cup sour cream	2 teaspoons parsley

Melt the butter in a heavy 12-inch skillet over high heat. When it gives off a nutty aroma, lower the heat and add the onions, finely chopped. Cook for 5 minutes or until the onions are golden brown.

Stir in the milkweed stalks, finely chopped, and cook over medium heat for 10 minutes or until tender. Add the sour cream, lemon juice and the salt and pepper. Cook, being careful not to boil, until the sour cream is heated through. Garnish with finely chopped parsley and serve at once.

MILKWEED STALKS WITH HAM AND CHEESE

8 large peeled milkweed stalks	1 teaspoon salt
1 cup milk	8 thin slices smoked ham
1 cup cold water	8 slices process cheese

Clean and peel the milkweed stalks and cut into 3-inch lengths. Arrange in the bottom of a 12-inch skillet and pour the milk and water over them. Put on the stove over medium heat. When small bubbles appear around the edges of the pan, reduce the heat to low, cover the pan tightly and simmer for 15 minutes.

Preheat the oven to 425°. Remove the milkweed stalks from the pan with tongs and drain on a bed of double paper towels. Wrap each stalk with a slice of ham and on top of the ham a slice of cheese. Butter an 8 by 10-inch baking dish and arrange the milkweed rolls side by side in it. Bake for 15 minutes, until the cheese has melted. Serve at once, directly from the baking pan.

STEAMED AND BUTTERED MILKWEED STALKS

1 pound milkweed stalks	4 tablespoons butter
5 cups water	1 teaspoon salt

Clean and peel the young milkweed stalks and rinse under running water. Pour the water into a large, heavy pot. It should come 1½ inches up the sides. Place a heatproof bowl upside down in the pot and a plate with the cleaned milkweed stalks on top of the bowl. Bring the water to a boil. Cover the pot tightly and steam for 10 minutes.

In a heavy 10-inch skillet melt the butter over a high heat. When it gives off a nutty aroma, reduce the heat. With tongs transfer the milkweed stalks from the plate on which they were steamed to the skillet. Turn the stalks in the butter, making sure they are well coated. Remove from the skillet and place on a heated serving platter. Serve at once when all the stalks are done. Sprinkle lightly with the salt.

YOUNG MILKWEED STALKS BRAISED WITH WILD ONIONS

1 pound young milkweed stalks	½ cup water
6 tablespoons butter	½ teaspoon salt
12 finely chopped wild onions	½ teaspoon sugar
6 wild leeks, finely chopped	2 tablespoons soft butter

Clean and peel the milkweed stalks and cut into ¼-inch pieces. Melt the butter over high heat in a heavy 3-quart saucepan and when it gives off a nutty aroma, lower the heat and add the onions. Cook for 5 minutes or until the onions are golden brown. Add the milkweed stalks, leeks and water. Season with the salt and sugar and simmer for 30 minutes while stirring occasionally. Let the fluid nearly evaporate. When the pot is almost dry, shake the mixture and stir in the soft butter. Serve in individual small bowls with any meat dish.

GLAZED MILKWEED STALKS

12 young milkweed stalks	½ teaspoon salt
1½ cups chicken stock	¼ teaspoon pepper
4 tablespoons butter	2 tablespoons finely chopped
2 tablespoons sugar	parsley

Clean and peel the young milkweed stalks and cut into 2-inch lengths. In a 12-inch skillet combine the stock, butter, sugar, salt, pepper and the milkweed stalks. Bring to a boil over moderate heat.

Cover the skillet and simmer over low heat. Shake the pan occasionally to roll the milkweed stalks about in the liquid. Cook for 20 minutes, making sure the liquid is not cooking away too fast. When the milkweed stalks are tender and the cooking fluid is brown and shiny, the dish is ready to remove from the stove. Before serving, roll the milkweed stalks around in the pan to assure that they are well coated. Transfer to a serving dish, sprinkle with parsley, and serve at once.

STEWED MILKWEED PODS WITH FROGS' LEGS

1 pound milkweed pods	12 pairs of frogs' legs
3 tablespoons butter	2 cups milk
3 tablespoons flour	½ teaspoon salt
1½ cups milk	Pepper
Juice of 1 lemon	1½ cups flour
½ teaspoon salt	Vegetable oil for deep-frying
¼ teaspoon white pepper	

Clean and wash the milkweed pods under running water and cut into ½-inch lengths. In a 2-quart saucepan bring 2 cups of water to a boil and add the milkweed pods. Boil for 5 minutes. Dump the pods into cold water and leave for 2 minutes. Drain well in a large sieve and set aside.

In a heavy 8 to 10-inch skillet melt the butter over high heat. When it gives off a nutty aroma lower the heat, stir in the flour and mix thoroughly. Pour in the milk while stirring constantly and continue stirring until the sauce starts to thicken and comes to a boil. Reduce the heat and simmer for 3 minutes. Add the milkweed pods to the sauce, add the lemon juice, salt and pepper and simmer over very low heat.

Wash the frogs' legs under cold running water. Dry them thoroughly with paper towels and set aside. In a small bowl mix the milk, salt and pepper, and soak the frogs' legs in the mixture for 10 minutes. Spread the flour on a sheet of wax paper.

In a heavy 12-inch skillet heat the oil over high heat until a light haze forms above it. Roll the frogs' legs in the flour and fry them in the hot oil for 7 minutes. Turn them frequently to brown on all sides. When they are golden brown, remove from the oil with tongs and place on paper towels to drain. Remove the bones and place the meat in a 4 by 8-inch baking dish. Pour the milkweed stew over them and serve at once. Garnish with slices of lemon.

BAKED MILKWEED STALKS OMELET

1 cup milkweed stalks	½ teaspoon salt
4 eggs	2 tablespoons olive oil

Preheat the oven to 425°. Clean and peel the milkweed stalks and cut in 5-inch lengths. Split the stalks lengthwise. To a 2-quart saucepan add 3 cups of water and bring to a boil over high heat. Add the milkweed stalks and boil for 5 minutes. Remove from heat and plunge into cold water. Drain through a large sieve and set aside.

In a small bowl beat the eggs till they are frothy. Add salt and set aside. Heat the olive oil in a 10-inch heavy skillet. Drop the milkweed stalks into the skillet and cook them over moderate heat for 5 minutes or until they are golden brown. Spread them over the bottom of a 1-quart casserole well greased with butter. Pour the eggs on top and bake in the upper half of the oven for 15 minutes or until the omelet is well set and the top golden brown.

STEAMED MILKWEED STALKS WITH BRANDY BUTTER

1 pound young milkweed stalks	½ cup sugar
5 cups water	½ teaspoon vanilla extract
1 teaspoon salt	4 tablespoons brandy
4 tablespoons butter	3 tablespoons butter

Peel and clean the milkweed stalks. Cut into 3-inch lengths. To a 3-quart heavy saucepan add the water and salt. Bring to a boil over high heat. Add the milkweed stalks and boil for 10 minutes. Remove from heat and drain well in a large sieve.

Combine 4 tablespoons butter, sugar, brandy and vanilla in a large bowl and beat with an electric beater until the mixture is smooth and well blended.

In another bowl beat remaining butter until it is light and fluffy. Beat the sugar mixture into the butter a little at a time and continue beating until the mixture is well blended and is white and frothy. Refrigerate for 3 hours or until firm. Reheat the milkweed stalks by placing the sieve over boiling water. Let the milkweed stalks stand over the steam for 4 to 5 minutes or until they are heated through. Place on a heated platter and spread half the brandy butter evenly over them. Serve the remaining butter in small individual cups.

MILKWEED PODS AND CHICKEN PIE

4-pound stewing fowl	1 pound milkweed pods, cleaned
3 wild onions, peeled and	and cut into pieces crosswise
quartered	8 slices bacon
2 2-inch pieces milkweed stalk	1 cup fresh bread crumbs
1 tablespoon salt	1 cup milk
½ teaspoon pepper	1 egg yolk
	½ cup heavy cream

In a heavy soup pot combine the fowl, onion, milkweed stalk, salt and pepper. Use enough cold water to cover the chicken by ½ inch. Bring to a boil over high heat. Skim off all the foam and scum with a large spoon. Reduce the heat and simmer until the fowl is tender but not falling apart.

Transfer the fowl to a plate and strain the stock through a fine sieve set over a large bowl. Press down hard on the vegetables with a large wooden spoon.

Pour 2 cups of the stock into a heavy 3-quart saucepan and skim the surface of all its fat. Add the milkweed pods and bring to a boil over high heat. Reduce the heat and simmer for 20 minutes. Remove from heat and set aside.

Skin the fowl and remove the meat from the bones. Cut it into 1-inch pieces and arrange them evenly on the bottom of a 2-quart casserole. Pour the milkweed pods over the top of the chicken, together with the stock.

In an 8-inch heavy skillet fry the bacon for 5 minutes over high heat. With tongs remove the bacon from the skillet and place it on top of the casserole.

In a small mixing bowl soak the bread crumbs in the milk, using a whisk to beat the mixture together. Spread on top of the casserole.

Preheat the oven to 425°. Beat the egg yolk until fluffy and add the heavy cream a little at a time. Add the mixture to the casserole, reserving ¼ cup. Place the casserole in the oven and bake for 1 hour. From time to time remove the casserole and using a pastry brush, brush some of the egg mixture on top of the pie. The top should turn golden brown and be soft. Serve the dish from the casserole.

MINT

(Mentha)

This plant is characterized by the square stems, opposite simple leaves and small purple, white or pink two-lipped auxiliary flowers in whorls which often form terminal spikes. All mints are noted for the fragrance of their foliage. The most common in North America are Canada mint *(Mentha arvensis)*, spearmint *(Mentha spicata)* and peppermint *(Mentha piperita)*.

MINT

You will find all three growing wild in the bush. When you come upon a patch, you cannot miss the refreshing aroma of this plant. Many a time when hunting or fishing I have enjoyed an improvised mint julep.

During survival courses in the bush, I teach my students to use the mint as much as possible for flavoring all sorts of dishes that would otherwise be flat or distasteful. For instance, boiled snake in mint sauce is a delicacy surpassed by few other dishes in the bush.

The Indians used mint to make wild vinegar, which has an agreeableness of its own. Mint leaves shredded and put into any salad improve the flavor, and mint also complements lamb and venison.

IN THE BUSH

The young leaves can be eaten raw with salt. Mint can also be cooked like any fresh vegetable.

Many years ago on a survival trip with an Indian friend, he gave me a lecture on how to cook vegetables that I will never forget. After watching me prepare green vegetables, he accused me of trying to kill them by over-cooking. Then he told me that vegetables should cook only as long as it takes you to turn around in front of the fire. After this trip, I have enjoyed my vegetables a great deal more by observing his advice.

As a Cooked Vegetable: Pluck and wash the mint leaves, boil in salt water for 2 or 3 minutes.

As Tea: A delicious tea can be prepared by boiling or steeping the fresh, clean leaves in boiling water. This tea is well-known in the United States and Canada.

As an Herb: Collect the leaves and dry them in the sun or in a 175° oven at home. They can then be preserved for a long time.

HOME RECIPES

MINT AND MILKWEED PODS SOUP

2 cups young milkweed pods	1 teaspoon salt
2 quarts chicken broth	¼ teaspoon pepper
1 cup wild onions, coarsely chopped	1 cup chopped mint
	1 cup heavy cream, chilled
¼ teaspoon ground cloves	3 or 4 sprigs of mint
1 bay leaf	

Wash the milkweed pods thoroughly under running cold water. Discard any that are dark and discolored. In a 5-quart soup kettle bring the chicken stock to a boil. Drop in the pods slowly so that the water never stops boiling. Add the onions, cloves, bay leaf, salt, pepper and mint. Reduce heat and simmer with the pan partially covered for an hour. Remove bay leaf.

Purée the soup through a food mill or a fine sieve over a large bowl. Then rub it through the sieve again back into the kettle. Season to taste. Don't forget to overseason it a bit, as the seasoning will be less noticeable when chilled. Put the soup back into the bowl and refrigerate for at least 4 hours. Before serving, stir in the chilled cream, thinning to suit yourself.

Taste for seasoning again and add the sprigs of mint.

MINT-STUFFED ROAST LEG OF LAMB

4-pound leg of lamb	4 wild leeks, finely chopped
6 slices bacon, finely chopped	4 stalks young bulrush shoots,
2 cups coarsely chopped mint	finely chopped
½ teaspoon salt	4 tablespoons margarine, melted
¼ teaspoon pepper	2 tablespoons flour
4 wild onions, finely chopped	2 cups beef stock

Remove the rump and leg bone, and I usually take out the shank bone as well. This will create a deep pocket for the stuffing. Do not remove the fell (skin) from the outside of the lamb.

Using a large mixing bowl, combine the bacon, mint, salt, pepper, onions, wild leeks and bulrush shoots. Mix thoroughly.

Fill the pocket in the lamb with the stuffing, making sure the cavity is full. Sew up the opening, then tie the leg at 2-inch intervals so it will keep its shape while cooking.

Preheat the oven to 500°. With a pastry brush coat lamb with the melted margarine and place it, fat side up, on a rack in a roasting pan.

Roast the leg uncovered in the middle of the oven for 20 minutes, basting from time to time with the juice from the bottom of the pan. Lower the heat to 400° and turn the leg over onto the other side. Sprinkle the lamb with finely chopped mint and salt and a few grindings of pepper. Roast for about an hour or if you like it well done, a little longer.

Transfer the leg to a heated platter and set aside.

Skim the fat off the top of the juices in the pan and add 2 tablespoons flour. Stir until the flour is smooth and free of lumps. Add a little milk and bring to a boil on top of the stove. Cook for 2 minutes or until the gravy is smooth. Add the beef stock and cook for 10 minutes or until the gravy has thickened. Taste for seasoning.

Pour gravy through a sieve and serve in a gravy boat with the carved lamb.

FRIED SMELTS WITH MINT AND PARSLEY BUTTER

8 tablespoons soft butter	20 smelts
½ teaspoon salt	1 cup flour
¼ teaspoon pepper	2 teaspoons salt
1 tablespoon parsley, finely	1 teaspoon pepper
chopped	2 cups vegetable shortening
2 tablespoons mint, finely	
chopped	

Cream the butter in a blender or with an electric beater until it is smooth and fluffy. Beat in the salt, pepper, parsley and mint.

Place the butter on a large strip of wax paper. Fold the paper and make a cylinder of the butter. It should be about ½ inch in diameter. Place in the refrigerator for at least 1½ hours.

Wash the smelts under cold running water and drain on a double thickness of paper towels. Take the heads and tails off with a sharp knife and with the tip of the knife, remove the backbone.

In a small paper bag, mix 1 cup of flour, 2 teaspoons salt and 1 teaspoon pepper. Close the bag and shake well to mix. Drop in 5 or 6 smelts at a time, close the bag and shake well. Put the floured smelts on a plate, making sure to remove the excess flour.

Heat the shortening in a 10-inch skillet over high heat until a light haze forms over it. Add as many of the smelts as the pan will hold. The fish should be opened out before being put into the pan. Cook for 4 minutes over moderate heat or until the fish are golden brown. Remove them to a double thickness of paper towels on a heated platter and keep warm in a low oven until all the fish are done.

Place the fish on a serving platter, spread open, skin side down. Remove butter from refrigerator, cut into ¼-inch slices and place in the middle of the fish. Use about 3 pieces of butter for each fish.

Place another fish on top of the first one, skin side up. Finish all the fish in this manner and serve as soon as possible, before the butter melts.

MINT-JELLIED EEL

3-pound eel	10 whole peppercorns
2 tablespoons coarse salt	2 teaspoons salt
2½ cups water	2 bay leaves
¼ cup white wine	¼ cup fresh lemon juice
2 wild onions, chopped finely	2 tablespoons mint, finely
1 cup mint, finely chopped	chopped

Skin the eel. An easy way to do this is to make a shallow cut around the neck behind the fins, wrap the head in a piece of newspaper, grab the skin with a pair of pliers and pull towards the tail. Then slit the eel open and remove the entrails.

Cut the eel in 2-inch pieces and wash well under running water. Place in a single layer in a shallow pan. Sprinkle with coarse salt and pour in enough boiling water to cover the pieces completely. Soak for 10 minutes, drain, and rinse thoroughly under cold running water.

Place the eel in a heavy 4 to 5-quart saucepan. Add the water, wine, onion, mint, peppercorns, salt and the bay leaves, and bring to a boil over high heat. Reduce the heat and simmer for 20 minutes. Remove the eel with a slotted spoon and transfer to a 10 by 12-inch baking dish. Pour the cooking juice through a sieve over the eel, stir in the lemon juice and sprinkle the freshly chopped mint on top. Refrigerate for at least 5 hours.

When thoroughly chilled, the liquid should form a soft jelly.

Serve from the baking dish.

POTATOES IN MINT SAUCE

6 small potatoes	1 teaspoon salt
5 tablespoons olive oil	½ teaspoon pepper
½ cup wild onions, finely chopped	1½ cups boiling water
1 teaspoon leeks, finely chopped	Mint sauce
4 tablespoons mint, finely chopped	

Peel and slice the potatoes crosswise into ½-inch rounds. In a heavy 12-inch skillet, heat the olive oil over high heat until a light haze forms above it. Add the potatoes, turning frequently with a slotted spoon for 10 minutes or until golden brown. Scatter the onions and leeks on top of the potatoes, stir and cook for 8 minutes. Add the mint, the salt and pepper and the water. Shake the pan back and forth to distribute the ingredients evenly.

Cover the skillet and simmer over low heat for 30 minutes. Make sure the potatoes do not stick to the pan. Remove the potatoes from the skillet with a slotted spoon and arrange on a heated serving platter.

Pour the rest of the contents over the potatoes and serve hot with the following cold sauce.

MINT SAUCE

½ cup hot water	¼ cup white wine
3 tablespoons sugar	½ cup mint, finely chopped

In a large bowl, mix the water, sugar and wine. Stir until the sugar dissolves completely. Add the mint leaves and let stand for at least 2 hours.

MOTHER'S MINT JELLY

3 cups fresh mint leaves	5 drops green food coloring
3 cups water	3½ cups sugar
2 tablespoons lemon juice	½ bottle fruit pectin

Wash the mint leaves under running water and remove any wilted or bruised leaves. Shred into small pieces to release the oil.

In a large 4 to 5-quart saucepan, bring the water to a boil over high heat. Add the mint leaves and cook for 2 minutes. Remove from heat, cover, and let steep for at least 10 minutes.

Wash the saucepan. Measure 1¾ cups of strained mint juice into it, add 2 tablespoons strained lemon juice, the food coloring and the sugar. Place the pan over low heat to dissolve sugar. Increase the heat and bring the mixture to a boil, stirring constantly. Add the fruit pectin all at once and bring to a full rolling boil for 1 minute, still stirring. Remove from heat.

Remove all the scum from the surface with a metal spoon. Pour into sterilized jelly jars immediately.

Cover the surface quickly with ⅛ inch of melted paraffin. Cool and store in fruit cellar.

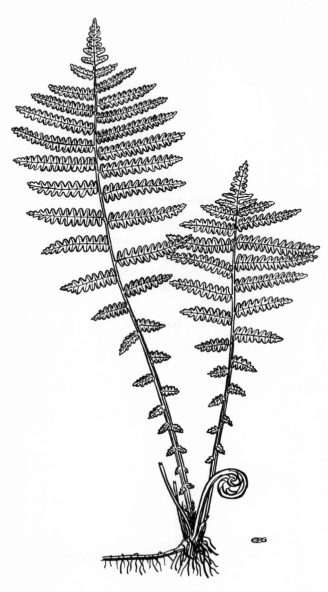

OSTRICH FERN

OSTRICH FERN

(Matteuccia struthiopteris)

The sterile fronds of this plant form circular clumps. The leaves are pinnately divided and not unlike ostrich plumes, a resemblance which has given the plant its name. The fertile fronds are somewhat comblike, and the sterile fronds can reach a height of 8 to 10 feet. The ostrich fern prefers rich soil near riverbanks, on fertile slopes or in woods.

The fern is a perennial with a dark brownish or almost black root. It is very much favored by the Japanese for flavoring soups and salads. As a matter of fact, it is so much in demand that the Japanese government has passed a law protecting the plant.

The part of this plant we pick is the fiddlehead, so called because of its resemblance to the tuning end of a violin. Fiddleheads should be picked before they reach the height of 5 to 6 inches and are still curled and rusty. Break them off with your fingers as low as possible.

Remove the loose brown coating by rubbing them between your hands, and then they are ready for preparation.

IN THE BUSH

As a Fresh Vegetable: The fiddleheads are edible just as you pick them. Simply clean and eat.

As a Cooked Vegetable: Pick the young curled fiddleheads, snip off the leafy portion and remove all the fuzz from the stem. Put them in boiling salted water and simmer for 10 minutes. Serve with drippings from the frying pan or with butter if you have it.

HOME RECIPES

FIDDLEHEADS WITH CHEESE AND BLACK BUTTER

24 fiddleheads   Black butter
Parmesan cheese

In a 3-quart saucepan place the fiddleheads with a little salt and enough water to cover, and boil for 10 minutes. Remove from heat and drain

65

thoroughly. On a long buttered dish sprinkled with grated Parmesan cheese, arrange fiddleheads in layers and sprinkle cheese between the layers.

When ready to serve, cover the cheese-sprinkled ferns copiously with black butter and set to glaze under the grill in the oven.

BLACK BUTTER

½ cup butter	Chopped parsley

Put ½ cup butter in a saucepan and cook until it is brown and begins to smoke. Add the chopped parsley and spread the mixture over the cheese-covered fiddleheads.

CREAM OF FIDDLEHEAD SOUP WITH MUSHROOMS

1 pound fiddleheads	1 can beef consommé
1 can cream of mushroom soup	1 teaspoon salt
2 cups milk	½ teaspoon pepper

Clean the rust and woolly coating from the fiddleheads by rubbing them between the hands, and wash under running water.

In a heavy 2-quart saucepan bring 1 quart of water and a teaspoon of salt to the boil. Drop the greens into the water and boil for 10 minutes. Remove from heat and immerse in cold water for 2 minutes. Drain and set aside.

Clean the saucepan and bring the mushroom soup and milk to a slow boil. Add fiddleheads and cook for 20 minutes over low heat. Place a fine sieve over a large bowl and pour the hot soup through. With a wooden spoon rub the mushrooms and fiddleheads through as well. Pour mixture from bowl back into the saucepan, add the consommé and simmer over low heat for 5 minutes.

Taste for seasoning, and if too thick, add a little milk.

Garnish with small pieces of fiddleheads and chopped parsley.

BRAISED FIDDLEHEADS

1 pound fiddleheads	½ cup thinly sliced onions
3 quarts water	1 cup beef stock
1 teaspoon salt	1 bay leaf
½ teaspoon pepper	2 tablespoons soft butter
8 slices bacon	2 tablespoons finely chopped
2 tablespoons butter	parsley

Remove the brown coating on the fiddleheads by rubbing them between your hands. Wash under running water to remove any trace of sand. Bring the water to a boil in a soup kettle. Drop the fiddleheads into the water and cook for 2 to 3 minutes.

Remove immediately with a slotted spoon and plunge them into cold water for 2 to 3 minutes. Gently squeeze in a large sieve to remove as much water as possible. Season with salt and pepper and set aside.

Preheat the oven to 350°. Cut the bacon crosswise in ¼-inch strips. In a 10-inch heavy skillet, heat 1 tablespoon of butter over high heat until it gives off a nutty aroma. Reduce heat, add the bacon and cook for 5 minutes.

Remove bacon with a slotted spoon and set aside. Increase heat, add the onions and cook till they are golden brown.

In a flameproof casserole melt the rest of the butter over low heat on top of the stove. Spread the onions on the bottom of the dish and place the fiddleheads evenly on top of them. Spread the bacon slices on top, add the beef stock and put bay leaf on top of mixture. Bring to a simmer on top of the stove, then cover tightly and bake in the lower part of the oven for 1½ hours.

Remove from oven, spread the soft butter on top and sprinkle with chopped parsley. Serve at once.

STEAMED FIDDLEHEADS IN WINE

2 pounds fiddleheads	2 cups white wine
½ teaspoon pepper	4 tablespoons melted butter
½ teaspoon salt	

Remove the brown coating on the fiddleheads by rubbing between your hands. Wash under running water. Pour enough water into a large heavy pot to come 1½ inches up the sides. Set a heatproof bowl upside down in the pot and place a plate on the bowl. Place the fiddleheads on the plate and sprinkle with the salt and pepper.

Add the wine to the water, cover tightly and boil for 15 minutes or until fiddleheads are soft. Carefully take fiddleheads from plate with tongs or a slotted spoon and place on hot platter. Pour melted butter over them and toss until they are well coated with butter. Serve at once.

BAKED EGGS WITH FIDDLEHEADS AND MEAT

1 pound young fiddleheads	1 tablespoon finely chopped
6 tablespoons butter	parsley
½ cup finely chopped wild onion	1 teaspoon salt
½ cup finely chopped smoked	½ teaspoon pepper
ham	6 eggs
3 pepperoni sausages cut in ¼-	3 tablespoons pale dry sherry
inch pieces	

Remove the rusty parts from the fiddleheads and wash under cold running water. Using a heavy 2 to 3-quart saucepan, boil the fiddleheads in a quart of salted water for 3 minutes. Remove from heat and plunge them in cold water for 2 to 3 minutes, drain in a coarse sieve and set aside.

Put a 12-inch skillet over high heat and melt 4 tablespoons of butter. When it smells slightly nutty, reduce heat and add the onion. Cook until golden brown. Add the smoked ham and pepperoni and cook over low heat for 5 minutes. Add parsley and seasonings.

Remove ½ cup of fiddleheads from the lot and set aside. Add the rest to the skillet and with constant stirring, cook for 10 minutes or until they are coated on all sides with the meat and onion mixture and most of the cooking fluid has evaporated.

Preheat oven to 425°. Using a pastry brush, coat the sides and bottom of a 9-inch baking dish with the rest of the butter. Spread the mixture from the skillet evenly in the dish. One at a time, break the eggs and drop carefully over the mixture. If you are not sure you can do this, break the eggs into a saucer and slide them off gently. Place the saved fiddleheads decoratively around the top of the dish and sprinkle the sherry over the eggs and vegetable.

Cover the dish and bake in the middle of the oven for 20 minutes or until the egg whites are firm and an opaque film has formed over the yolks. Serve at once.

FIDDLEHEAD ICE CREAM

1 pint vanilla ice cream	2 to 5 tablespoons milk
12 fiddleheads	Whipped cream

Set the ice cream to melt at room temperature in a large mixing bowl. Parboil the fiddleheads for 5 minutes, then drain thoroughly. Quickly pound them to a pulp together with enough milk to make the consistency of thick batter. Put in a saucepan and let it come to a boil over moderate heat.

Steep for 20 minutes, then strain the liquid into the bowl with the melted ice cream. Stir thoroughly, put into individual sherbert glasses and freeze for at least 3 hours before serving.

Garnish with a dot of whipped cream.

ROAST GOOSE WITH FIDDLEHEAD STUFFING

4 pounds fiddleheads	3 cups chopped wild onions
1 orange	2 cups finely chopped crabapples
1 cup grated arrowhead tubers	1 tablespoon caraway seeds
6 tablespoons butter	8 to 10-pound goose
	Salt and pepper

Preheat the oven to 350°. Remove the brown coating on the fiddleheads by rubbing between your hands. Wash under cold running water.

Peel the orange and squeeze juice into a large mixing bowl, removing all seeds. Peel the arrowhead tubers and grate very fine to make 1 cup. Add to the orange juice and stir well to be sure that the grated tubers are thoroughly coated with juice.

Heat the butter over high heat in a 12-inch skillet until it gives off a nutty odor, reduce heat and add the onions. Cook until onions are golden brown, add fiddleheads, apples and the caraway seeds. Let simmer for 10 minutes, stirring occasionally. Transfer mixture to the mixing bowl with the tubers and the orange.

Wash the goose inside and out, and pat dry. Sprinkle the cavity generously with salt and pepper. Fill the goose with the fiddlehead stuffing, sew up the openings with needle and thread, and truss the legs with cord. Set the goose, breast side up, on a rack in a large roasting pan. Cook in the middle of the oven for 2½ hours or 25 minutes a pound. With a bulb baster, remove all the fat that drips into the pan. The goose is ready when the juice from a punctured thigh runs pale yellow.

Remove to a serving platter and cut away the thread and cord. Transfer the stuffing to a serving dish. Let the goose rest for at least 20 minutes before carving it.

PURÉED FIDDLEHEADS WITH SMOKED PORK

½ teaspoon salt
  2-pound smoked pork butt
1 pound fiddleheads
4 slices bacon

½ cup minced wild onions
3 cups chicken stock
4 arrowhead roots
½ cup cream

Fill a 4 to 5-quart soup kettle with 3 quarts of water, add the salt and place over high heat. When the water boils reduce the heat, put in the pork butt and let it simmer covered for 1½ hours.

Remove the brown coating from the fiddleheads by rubbing them between your hands, and wash under cold running water.

In a heavy 2-quart saucepan, cook the bacon until the fat is rendered and the bacon is lightly browned. Remove bacon with a slotted spoon and set aside. Add the finely chopped onions and cook till they are golden. Pour in the chicken stock, add the peeled and diced arrowhead roots and the reserved bacon. Season to taste. Bring stock to a boil and reduce the heat to a low simmer. Cover the pot tightly and simmer for 1½ hours or until the fiddleheads and the arrowhead roots are soft and easily mashed. Then pour the entire contents of the pot into a large sieve and with the back of a wooden spoon press through the sieve into a large mixing bowl.

Return the purée to the saucepan, add the cream and turn the heat to the lowest point. Cover and simmer for 5 or 6 minutes. Seasoning is now necessary.

Carve the pork butt into ¼-inch slices and arrange on a platter. Serve the purée in a large sauceboat.

PURSLANE

PURSLANE
(Portulaca oleracea)

Purslane is thought to be a native of Persia, where it was used as a common potherb more than 2,000 years ago. Its very branching stems hug the ground, and are smooth, reddish colored and succulent. The light green leaves are broad at the tips and taper towards the base, with a thick, smooth and fleshy texture. The flowers are small, yellow and five petaled. The seed capsules contain many flat, oval black seeds. As many as 50,000 seeds have been counted on a single plant.

IN THE BUSH

As a Fresh Vegetable: The juicy, slightly sour stems and leaves are very good eaten raw. They are also good as a thirst quencher because of their high water content.

As a Mush: With a great deal of patience and perseverance, enough seeds can be gathered and ground up and boiled into a mush, a practice once common among the Indians of North America.

As a Pickled Vegetable: In the days of the Pilgrims, purslane was frequently pickled and in that manner preserved for long periods.

PICKLED PURSLANE

To make juice for pickling. Dig into a red ant hill and collect as many ants as you can. Put them into a pot of boiling water together with two wild onions. Simmer for one hour. Strain off the juice and cool. Make a container out of birch bark and seal it with pitch from an evergreen. Fill the container ¾ full of the juice and fill up with purslane leaves and stems. Put a lid on the container and seal with pitch. Store in a cool place.

PURSLANE SALAD

An excellent salad can be made out of purslane leaves, mint and watercress. As salad dressing, use boiled-down sap from the sugar maple.

71

HOME RECIPES

BACON-COATED PURSLANE

6 slices bacon	1 pound purslane tips
½ cup water	Salt and pepper
½ cup vinegar	2 eggs, hard-boiled
4 teaspoons brown sugar	

Cut the bacon into small shreds and fry them very crisp. Add the water, vinegar and brown sugar. Simmer on low heat for 10 minutes. Stir constantly to prevent the sugar from burning.

Clean and wash the young, tender purslane tips. Add them to the mixture and stir gently so the tips are well coated. Season, garnish with the finely chopped eggs, and serve hot.

PICKLED PURSLANE

2 cups salt	3 sticks cinnamon
4 cups sugar	A few whole cloves
½ cup ground mustard seeds	4 quarts purslane tips
4 quarts vinegar	

In a saucepan mix the salt, sugar, mustard and vinegar over slow heat, stirring all the time. Tie the cinnamon sticks and cloves in cheesecloth and add to the brine just before it is taken off the heat. Put the purslane tips in a crock and pour the brine over, leaving in the cinnamon and cloves. Cover with a weighted plate and leave for at least 3 to 4 weeks. This pickle, used by the Pilgrims as a daily dish, will really make your friends marvel.

PURSLANE MOLD

6 tablespoons butter	3 egg yolks
2 tablespoons dry bread crumbs	¼ cup freshly grated cheese
3 tablespoons minced wild onions	½ teaspoon salt
¾ pound purslane leaves	½ teaspoon pepper
3 tablespoons flour	3 egg whites
1 cup milk	

Preheat the oven to 325°. Put 2 tablespoons of butter into a metal mold which has a cover and place in the oven. When the butter is melted, use a pastry brush to coat the bottom and sides of the mold with it. Dust the inside of the mold with the bread crumbs and tap the pan lightly to knock out any excess. Place a heavy 12-inch skillet over high heat and add 2 tablespoons of butter. When the butter gives off a nutty aroma, reduce the heat and stir in the finely chopped onions. Cook over moderate heat for 10 to 12 minutes, stirring frequently, until the onions are transparent but not brown. Add the washed and cleaned purslane leaves, stirring constantly for 4 to 5 minutes. When all the moisture has evaporated and the purslane leaves start to stick to the pan, remove the skillet from the heat.

Melt the remaining 2 tablespoons of butter in a heavy 3 to 4-quart saucepan. Remove from the heat and stir in the flour. Pour in the milk and with a wire whisk work the mixture into a smooth cream. Return the pan to low heat and cook for 5 minutes with constant stirring. Remove the pan from the heat and beat in the egg yolks one at a time, making sure each blends thoroughly before adding the next. Stir in the cheese, onions, purslane leaves and seasoning. Set aside to cool slightly. Beat the egg whites with an electric beater until they are very stiff. Stir a heaping tablespoon of egg whites into the sauce in order to lighten it and then fold in the rest of the egg whites. Pour the mixture into the buttered mold.

Place the mold in a pot. Add water to reach about ¾ of the way up the sides of the mold. Cover the pot and bake in the oven for 1 hour. To serve, wipe the outside dry. Run a knife or a narrow spatula around the inside of the mold. Place a serving plate upside down over the mold and, holding the two firmly together, invert. Rap the bottom of the form with the handle of a knife, and the mold should slide out easily. Serve at once.

SMALL PURSLANE DUMPLINGS

4 tablespoons butter	½ teaspoon salt
2 cups finely chopped purslane leaves	½ teaspoon pepper
	¼ teaspoon nutmeg
¾ cup old sharp cheese, grated	6 to 8 quarts water
2 eggs, lightly beaten	1 tablespoon salt
6 tablespoons flour	4 tablespoons butter
¾ cup Parmesan cheese	

Melt the butter in a 10-inch skillet over high heat. When it gives off a nutty aroma, lower the heat and add the purslane leaves. Cook for 4 to 5 minutes or until the leaves start to stick to the pan. Add the grated cheese and cook for another 5 minutes.

With a spatula or wooden spoon transfer the contents of the skillet into a large mixing bowl. Add the lightly beaten eggs, the flour, ¼ cup of the Parmesan cheese, the salt, pepper and nutmeg. Leave in a cool place or refrigerate for 1 hour.

Preheat the oven to 425°. Bring the water to a boil and add 1 tablespoon of salt. Reduce the heat and let the water simmer gently.

Remove the mixture from the refrigerator. Flour your hands lightly and form the chilled mixture into small balls, a tablespoon at a time. Using a slotted spoon, gently lower the balls into the simmering water and cook them uncovered for 10 minutes or until they are somewhat firm to touch. With the slotted spoon, remove from the water and set aside to drain on paper towels.

Melt 2 tablespoons of butter in a 8 by 10-inch casserole, using a pastry brush to make sure the bottom and sides are well greased.

Arrange a layer of balls in the dish, keeping them about ½ inch apart. Melt the remaining butter, pour it over them and sprinkle with the remaining Parmesan cheese.

Bake in the middle of the oven for 10 minutes or until the cheese melts and the balls are thoroughly heated. Serve this dish as hot as possible, with additional cheese as a complement.

SPICED PURSLANE LEAVES

2 pounds fresh purslane leaves	2 bay leaves
1 tablespoon bacon fat	¼ teaspoon caraway seeds
½ cup wild onions, finely chopped	½ pound Canadian bacon in one
2 tablespoons sugar	piece
2 cups water	3 arrowhead tubers
10 whole juniper berries	Salt and pepper
5 peppercorns	

Clean and wash the purslane leaves under running water. Squeeze the leaves and pat with paper towels until completely dry.

Melt the bacon fat in a 3-quart casserole over moderate heat. Add the chopped onions and cook for 10 to 12 minutes, stirring constantly until the onions are lightly browned. Add the purslane leaves, sugar and water. Mix thoroughly, separating the purslane leaves with a fork. Tie spices into a cheesecloth bag and drop into the casserole. Place the bacon on top. Bring to a boil over high heat, then reduce the heat and simmer for 25 minutes.

Scrape and peel the arrowhead tubers, grate them directly into the casserole and with a fork stir into the purslane leaves. Cover the casserole tightly and cook over low heat for 2 hours. Remove the bag of spices and discard. Season with salt and pepper to taste.

Remove the bacon and slice in ¼-inch slices. Heap the purslane leaves in the middle of a large heated platter. Surround with the bacon.

PURSLANE IN CREAM SAUCE

1 pound purslane leaves	1 cup milk
2 teaspoons salt	1 cup heavy cream
4 tablespoons butter	½ teaspoon pepper
4 tablespoons flour	

Clean and wash the purslane leaves under running water, making sure that sand and grit is removed. Squeeze to remove as much water as possible. Put a 4-quart heavy saucepan on medium heat and fill with 3 quarts of water. Add ½ teaspoon of salt. Shred the purslane leaves into the water and bring to a boil, lower the heat and cook for 15 minutes, well covered. Drain through a large sieve, pressing down hard on the leaves with a wooden spoon to remove all the water. Put the leaves on a board and chop very fine.

In a 2-quart heavy saucepan, melt the butter over high heat. When the butter gives off a nutty aroma, remove the pan from the heat and add the flour. Add the milk and cream all at once, stirring constantly. Replace the pan over the heat and stirring vigorously with a wire whisk, let the mixture come to a boil, lower the heat and cook for 10 minutes. Add the remaining salt, the pepper and the chopped purslane leaves. Cook for another 5 minutes or until the purslane leaves are heated through.

This dish can be served with roast pork or beef.

PURSLANE PANCAKES

½ pound fresh purslane leaves	2 tablespoons butter, melted
1½ cups milk	2 eggs
1 teaspoon salt	1 tablespoon sugar
¼ teaspoon nutmeg	2 tablespoons butter
1 cup flour	

Clean and wash the purslane leaves under running water. Drop them into a heavy 3 to 4-quart saucepan with water and a little salt and bring to a boil over high heat. Cook for 3 to 4 minutes, then drain and squeeze dry. Chop very finely on a chopping board. Set aside.

In a large mixing bowl combine the milk, salt, nutmeg and flour, mix well and then stir in 2 tablespoons of melted butter a little at a time. Mix the eggs and the sugar in a separate bowl, then stir into the batter. Stir into this the chopped purslane leaves, a little at a time.

Melt 1 tablespoon of butter in a heavy 12-inch skillet and with a pastry brush coat the sides of the skillet well. Place the pan over high heat and when hot, drop in 2 tablespoons of the batter and spread it out in a 3-inch disc. Cook the pancakes 3 or 4 at a time for 3 to 4 minutes on each side or until they have browned lightly. Keep them warm on a heated platter covered with aluminium foil until all the batter is used. Midway, the skillet will require regreasing with a last tablespoon of butter.

Serve pancakes hot, with cranberry sauce.

PURSLANE AND LIVER CASSEROLE

1½ pounds purslane leaves	2 tablespoons corn syrup
8 slices bacon	2 teaspoons salt
2 wild onions, finely chopped	¼ teaspoon pepper
2 cups heavy cream	1½ pounds beef liver
2 eggs, lightly beaten	2 tablespoons butter

Wash and clean the purslane leaves to remove all sand and grit. Put them in a 3-quart saucepan, cover with water, and add a pinch of salt. Bring to a boil and cook for 3 minutes. Drain the water and chop the purslane leaves finely. Set aside.

In a heavy 10-inch skillet cook the bacon over high heat until it is crisp and brown. With a slotted spoon remove bacon from the pan and set aside. Remove all fat from the skillet except a thin film in the bottom. Add the wild onions and cook for 5 minutes or until the onions are transparent but not brown. Remove from heat and set aside.

Preheat the oven to 375°. Using a large mixing bowl, combine the chopped purslane leaves, cream and the lightly beaten eggs. Mix well. Add the cooked onions, crumbled bacon, corn syrup, salt and pepper. Dry the beef liver with paper towels and slice thinly. Put the skillet on high heat and add the bacon fat. When the fat smokes, lower the heat and add the liver. Cook over medium heat for 10 minutes, turning the slices on both sides. When they are nicely browned, remove from the skillet and set aside.

In a 2-quart casserole melt 2 tablespoons of butter over medium heat.

When the butter is melted, coat the sides and the bottom of the casserole with a pastry brush. Pour in half the purslane mixture and place the thinly sliced liver on top, spread out in an even layer. Add the rest of the purslane mixture. Bake in the middle of the oven for 1 hour or until a knife inserted in the middle of the casserole comes out clean. Serve hot with cranberry sauce.

SHEEP SORREL

SHEEP SORREL

(Rumex acetosella)

The leaves of this plant are soft and light green in color and like the arrowhead in shape. The plant is smooth and erect, with dense clusters of reddish flowers. It is known also as sour grass and stands from 8 to 12 inches high. You will find it in waste places, dry fields, hillsides and on low land.

This plant was introduced from Europe but is now widespread in the United States and Canada. It can be easily recognized by the red pigment which appears in the roots and inflorescences, and often in the leaves. The leaves are distinctly sour tasting. The plant is one-sexed, and either pollen bearing or seed bearing.

Sheep sorrel was used by the early settlers in soups, salads and to make drinks. The leaves are delicious when mixed with other greens in a salad.

IN THE BUSH

I usually use the plant to make a sour thirst-quenching drink by cleaning the leaves and simmering them for 20 minutes in plenty of water. This makes a drink that has the taste of lemonade. It can be drunk either hot or cold.

HOME RECIPES

SHEEP SORREL PIE

1 **quart sheep sorrel leaves**	7 **egg whites**
2 **cups water**	1 **tablespoon confectioners' sugar**
7 **egg yolks**	**Pie shell**
¾ **cup sugar**	

Clean and wash the sheep sorrel leaves under running cold water. In a heavy 3 to 4-quart saucepan bring the water to a boil. Shred the sorrel leaves and add to the boiling water. Cook for 3 minutes. Remove from heat and let steep for at least ½ hour.

With a rotary or electric beater, beat the egg yolks for a minute, then slowly pour in ½ cup sugar. Beat until the mixture is thick and heavy. Stir in ½ cup of the strained juice of the sheep sorrel. Transfer the mixture into a small stainless steel saucepan. Stirring constantly, cook over low heat for about 5 minutes or until the mixture lightly coats a spoon. Do not allow it to boil or the eggs will curdle. Remove from heat and cool slightly.

Beat the egg whites until they are frothy. Slowly pour in the remaining sugar and continue to beat until the whites form stiff peaks. With a rubber spatula mix about a third of the whites into the egg yolk mixture, then gently but thoroughly fold in the rest. Set aside to cool to room temperature, and then place in the refrigerator.

PIE SHELL

1¼ cups all purpose flour	2 tablespoons butter
4 tablespoons chilled vegetable shortening	3 tablespoons water

Using a large mixing bowl, combine the flour, shortening, butter and salt. Using your fingertips, rub the flour and fat together until they look like coarse meal. Pour the water over, toss together, and knead gently with your hands until the dough can be gathered into a compact ball.

Dust with flour and chill the dough for at least 1 hour. Lightly butter a 9-inch pie plate. On a floured baking board roll out the dough into a circle about ¼-inch thick and 14 inches in diameter. Lift it up on the rolling pin and unroll over the pie plate, making sure it is fitted well down onto the pan. Trim the excess pastry with scissors to within ½ inch from the plate and fold the overhanging dough back to make a double thickness all around the rim. Using your fingers, press the pastry down around the rim.

Preheat the oven to 400°. Remove the filling from the refrigerator and with a rubber spatula fill the pie shell.

Bake in the center of the oven until the filling has firmed and lightly browned.

Cool at room temperature and before serving, dust with confectioners' sugar.

COLD SHEEP SORREL SOUFFLÉ

1 pound sheep sorrel leaves	8 egg whites
2 cups cold water	1 cup sugar
2 envelopes unflavored gelatin	1 cup heavy cream, chilled
1 cup cold water	3 tablespoons sugar
8 egg yolks	½ cup heavy cream, whipped

Clean the sheep sorrel leaves well and wash under running cold water. Place a 3 to 4-quart stainless steel saucepan over high heat and add the water. Add the leaves to the pan and bring to a boil. Cook for 5 minutes, remove from heat and let steep for at least 2 hours. Strain the leaves through a large sieve over a mixing bowl. Set aside.

Sprinkle the gelatin into the cup of cold water and let it soften. Using an electric beater, beat the egg yolks until they are thick. Beat in the softened gelatin.

Cook the mixture in a small stainless steel saucepan over low heat, stirring constantly until it thickens enough to coat a spoon slightly. Transfer into a large mixing bowl and stir in 1½ cups of the sheep sorrel juice. Place in the refrigerator for about ¾ of an hour.

Beat the egg whites until they begin to froth, then pour in the sugar slowly and beat until the whites are stiff. In another bowl, whip the chilled cream until it holds its shape and then stir in the 3 tablespoons sugar. With a spatula fold the cream gently but thoroughly into the sheep sorrel mixture, and then fold in the egg whites. Tie a wax paper collar around an 1½-quart soufflé dish. The paper should protrude at least 2 inches above the rim. Pour in the sheep sorrel mixture up to the top of the collar, smooth the top with a knife and refrigerate for at least 4 hours. Remove the collar and pipe decorations of whipped cream on top of the soufflé.

Serve chilled.

SHEEP SORREL LEMONADE

1 pound fresh sheep sorrel leaves	**1 cup sugar**
5 cups water	**20 ounces soda water**

Clean and discard any bruised leaves and wash thoroughly under cold running water. In a 3-quart heavy saucepan, bring the water to a boil. Add the sugar, stirring constantly until it is well dissolved. Add the sheep sorrel leaves, having first shredded them into small pieces. Boil for a few minutes and remove from heat. Place the lid on the saucepan and let steep for 2 or 3 hours.

Strain the mixture through a sieve into a large mixing bowl and place in the refrigerator for at least 2 hours. When ready to serve, pour the juice into a pitcher and add the soda water. Serve over ice in a large tumbler.

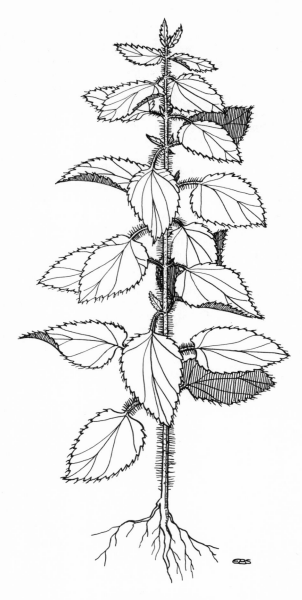

STINGING NETTLE

STINGING NETTLE
(Urtica spp.*)*

The plant is dark green with straight stems and green flower clusters. It varies in height from 2 to 4 feet. If you want to be really sure it is a stinging nettle, give the plant a swat with the back of your hand. Such rash action causes a painful stinging sensation in the skin. However, in a short time it will wear away.

Nettle leaves may be gathered in the spring and early summer. This unlikely but delectable food is one of the first greens to appear in the spring.

The memory of my grandfather roaming around behind our farmhouse early in the spring to collect this delicacy will always stay vivid in my memory, as well as the fresh spring soup which followed.

Grandfather was the hardy type and did not use any gloves, but I suggest that you wear gloves and use a knife when collecting this plant. You may wonder how in the world you can eat a plant that requires gloves to handle, but the leaves, and the whole plant for that matter, lose their stinging properties when boiled.

The Indians used to relieve nettle stings by rubbing the irritation with the dryish, rusty, feltlike material that covers fiddleheads.

IN THE BUSH

Obviously this is a vegetable you cannot eat raw, but one word of caution: Please do not overcook these delicately flavored greens.

When boiled, very young nettle shoots somewhat resemble beansprouts in flavor and texture. An old Indian let me in on a secret way to collect them. He pulled the plant out of the ground and cut off those pinkish shoots that grow below the surface, and then he prepared a **nettle stew** which I'll never forget.

He boiled 2 cups of the young shoots in ½ cup of water to which he added ½ cup of red ants and about 2 dozen minnows, heads and all. Believe me, this stew was delicious.

He also taught me to make a **nettle twine** out of dried stalks soaked in water. The outer skin was taken off, and the inner material twisted to make a twine which was unbelievably strong.

HOME RECIPES
FRESH STINGING NETTLE SOUP

3 cups water	2 egg yolks
2 pounds young stinging nettle leaves	1 cup heavy cream
	1 teaspoon salt
5 tablespoons butter	½ teaspoon white pepper
4 tablespoons flour	2 tablespoons soft butter
5 cups chicken stock	

In a 3 to 4-quart saucepan, bring the water to a boil. Drop the stinging nettle leaves in and remove immediately from the heat. Plunge the leaves into cold water and let sit for a minute or two. Drain the leaves through a large sieve and set aside.

Clean the saucepan and melt 5 tablespoons of butter over high heat. When the butter gives off a nutty aroma, lower the heat and, stirring constantly, add the flour. Cook for a minute, remove from heat and add the chicken stock. Place the pan on the heat and stir until the soup base is smooth and creamy. Simmer.

Take the well-drained nettle leaves and chop them into small pieces. In a small mixing bowl blend the egg yolks and the cream together, then whisk in 6 tablespoons of the simmering soup base. Reverse the process by whisking the egg mixture into the soup base. When the two are well blended, add the finely chopped nettle leaves and heat well. Do not let the soup come to a boil, as it will curdle.

Remove from heat and season with salt and pepper. Serve the soup from a tureen, with the soft butter floating on top.

BRAISED NETTLE SHOOTS AND PORK CHOPS IN CREAM SAUCE

2 cups very young nettle shoots	½ teaspoon pepper
2 cups water	4 tablespoons butter
6 inch-thick pork chops	1 cup heavy cream
½ teaspoon salt	

Clean the fresh nettle shoots thoroughly, making sure all earth is removed. In a 2 to 3-quart saucepan bring the water to a boil. Drop the nettle shoots into the water a few at a time so the water does not stop boiling. When they are all in, remove at once from heat and plunge the shoots into cold water. Let stand for a minute, then drain through a fine sieve. Set aside.

Preheat the oven to 350°. Season the chops with salt and pepper. Put a heavy 12-inch skillet over high heat and melt the butter. When it gives off a nutty odor, reduce the heat, add the chops 2 at a time, and brown them for about 4 minutes on each side or until they are golden brown. Remove from the skillet with tongs and place in a flameproof casserole large enough to hold all the chops in one layer.

Drain almost all the fat from the skillet and reserve in a small bowl. Put the nettle shoots into the skillet and cook for 3 to 4 minutes, making sure they are well coated on all sides. Place them on top of the pork chops.

Return the fat to the skillet and bring to a boil. When boiling, reduce the heat and add the heavy cream, stirring constantly. Make sure all browned bits that cling to the bottom of the skillet are mixed into the cream.

Pour the mixture from the skillet into the casserole. Bring to a boil on top of the stove. When boiling, cover tightly and place in the oven. Bake for 1 hour. Check the cooking fluid from time to time and if it seems to cook away too fast, add a couple of tablespoons of red wine.

Serve from the casserole.

DUCK STUFFED WITH NETTLE SHOOTS AND ORANGES

4 cups nettle shoots	4 tablespoons butter
5-pound duck	½ pound large prunes
Salt and pepper	1 cup chicken stock
4 oranges	½ cup heavy cream

Preheat the oven to 350°. Clean and wash the nettle shoots under cold water and set aside. Wash the duck under cold running water and dry with paper towels. Rub the cavity with salt and pepper. Put 2 cups of nettle shoots in a large mixing bowl. Peel 2 oranges, cut the pulp into small pieces and add to the shoots. Mix well and stuff the cavity of the duck with the mixture. Truss the duck.

In a heavy 12-inch skillet melt the butter over high heat. When it gives off a nutty odor, lower the heat and brown the duck on all sides, turning it with tongs or two spoons.

Drain all the juices from the skillet to a heavy roasting pan. Place the unsoaked prunes in the bottom as evenly as possible. Peel the remaining 2 oranges, cut the pulp coarsely and spread over the prunes. Place the duck on top, breast up. Cover the pan, place in the middle of the oven and cook for 1 hour.

Remove from the oven and transfer the duck to a plate. Strain the roasting juices through a fine sieve, pressing down slightly on the fruits with a wooden spoon so that all the juices are extracted. Discard the fruit.

Place the roasting pan on top of the stove, and after adding the fruit juices, bring to a boil. Add the chicken stock, stirring constantly. Remove from heat and add the heavy cream a little at a time. Mix well. Bring to a boil with constant stirring. Replace the duck in the roasting pan and add the remaining 2 cups of nettle shoots. Return to the oven and cook covered for 10 minutes. Remove the cover, increase the temperature to 500° and glaze for 5 minutes.

Place the duck on a heated serving platter. Remove the stuffing from the cavity and place around the duck with the nettle shoots.

Strain the pan juices through a fine sieve and serve in a gravy boat.

OPEN-FACED OMELET WITH NETTLE SHOOTS AND HAM

4 tablespoons butter	½ teaspoon pepper
2 cups nettle shoots	1 cup heavy cream
¼ pound smoked ham	½ cup flour
6 eggs	1 cup milk
1 teaspoon salt	

Preheat the oven to 425°. Wash the nettle shoots under cold running water. In a heavy 10-inch skillet melt the butter over high heat. When it gives off a nutty odor, reduce the heat and add the ham finely chopped. Cook for 5 minutes, remove the ham with a slotted spoon and set aside. Add the shoots to the skillet and cook for 5 minutes, then remove with a slotted spoon and set aside.

Grease a 2-quart casserole with butter. In a large mixing bowl combine the eggs, salt, pepper and the heavy cream. Using an electric beater, mix the ingredients well. Pour the contents of the mixing bowl into the casserole and place in the middle of the oven for 10 minutes.

Pour the fat from the skillet through a sieve into a saucepan. Add the flour, stirring constantly over medium heat. When the roux is smooth, add the milk and cook for 5 minutes with constant stirring. Add the nettle shoots and ham to the roux and stir gently so that all the ingredients are well mixed and the nettle shoots and ham are thoroughly heated.

Remove the casserole from the oven and spread the mixture evenly on top of the omelet. Bake for another 20 to 25 minutes until it is nicely browned.

If you wish to sprinkle sharp grated cheese on top, it will greatly improve the dish. Serve at once from the casserole.

THISTLE

THISTLE
(Cirsium vulgare)

The rosette leaves of this plant are large, deeply lobed, coarsely toothed and have sharp marginal pricklets. The upper surface of the leaves has short prickles, and the undersurface is covered with white hairs. The flowering stem is about 4 feet high, with prickly wings. The stem leaves are smaller than the rosette leaves, but otherwise similar. The flowers are all tubular and purplish.

The thistle is a native of Europe and Asia but emigrated to this continent with the early settlers, partly mixed in with agricultural seed. In Europe the thistle was used as a potherb and was well-known to the Greeks and the Romans.

Despite the unlikely appearance for an edible plant, this rough looking vegetable makes a delightful dish when properly prepared. My main reason for including it is its value as an emergency food. When the food supply is getting low, it is easy to recognize, and people scared of poisoned plants don't have to worry. The thistle is a pest in most parts of the country, so it should be no trouble to gather enough to live on for weeks. For instance, the Canada thistle occupies millions of acres of range and woodlands across the northern states and Canada. And the yellow star thistle is spreading in central California and threatens to ruin many thousand of acres of foothill pasture.

IN THE BUSH

As a Fresh Vegetable: The leaves are edible after the prickles have been removed, either raw or cooked. So are the stalks after the tough skin has been removed. A delightful salad can be made out of young thistle leaves and sliced tomatoes and hard-boiled eggs.

As a Cooked Vegetable: If you are in the bush without food, the best way to prepare thistles is to skin the stalks, cut them up into 2-inch pieces, and boil them in salted water. Many an explorer has survived by using thistles both as a diet and a material for making fishlines or snares.

To Make a Cord: Cut open the stalk and remove the fibers from the rind. Tie 2 fibers together and hook the loop over a peg. Holding the lines in either hand, twist each side over to the right, still twisting bring the right-hand fiber over to the left, and then the process is repeated and more fibers are used until you have the length of line required.

HOME RECIPES

BAKED FISH WITH BULL THISTLE STUFFING

3 tablespoons thistle stalk   ¼ teaspoon pepper
1 cup thistle leaves   4-pound lake trout
4 tablespoons butter   6 tablespoons soft butter
2 cups white bread crumbs   4 tablespoons heavy cream
½ teaspoon salt   1 cup dry white wine

Peel the stalk of its outer skin and chop in small pieces. Use the small stalk leaves from the thistle, and cut off the small prickles in the tip of the leaf with a sharp knife. Chop the leaves finely.

Using a heavy 10-inch stainless steel skillet, melt the butter over high heat and cook the chopped thistle stalks and leaves for about 3 minutes, making sure they are well covered with butter. Transfer to a large mixing bowl and add the bread crumbs, salt and pepper. Toss them all together.

Preheat the oven to 425°. Wash the fish inside and out under cold running water and pat dry with paper towels. Fill the fish with the stuffing, close the opening with small skewers and crisscross kitchen string as you would lace a turkey. Brush the bottom of a baking dish with 2 tablespoons of soft butter. Pour in the cream. Place the fish in the dish and brush the top with another 2 tablespoons soft butter. Sprinkle salt and pepper on top of the fish. Combine the rest of the melted butter and the wine and pour it around the fish. Bring to a simmer on top of the stove, then bake uncovered on the middle shelf in the oven for 45 minutes, basting every 8 to 10 minutes. Remove the pan from the oven and serve immediately. Garnish with a few sprigs of watercress if you have it.

WATERCRESS

(Nasturtium-aquaticum)

This plant is fleshy and succulent. Rooting occurs at the nodes in water. The leaves have somewhat rounded lobes, with the terminal lobe being the largest.

The leaves are a dark shiny green. The flowers are white and usually grow in clusters. The plant is widespread in rivers, brooks or springs in the eastern part of North America. It is found less frequently in the prairie region but increases on the west coast.

WATERCRESS

IN THE BUSH

As this plant grows in running water, the stream has pretty well washed the plant, so you can use it as it comes from nature.

When gathering watercress, do not pull up the whole plant but snip or pinch off the greens at the water's surface.

As a Fresh Vegetable: If you are fortunate enough to find this plant, just sit on the stream bank and pick handfuls of leaves and stems and eat them raw.

As a Salad: On early spring hiking trips, one of my favorite salads is made out of watercress, wood sorrel, purslane and wild onion. As salad dressing, I use the sap from the sugar maple or birch.

As a Cooked Vegetable: Watercress is particularly good in stew with rabbit and wild onion. Skin the rabbit, clean the carcass well, and cut up into small pieces. Put the meat in a small pot and fill with water, boil for 20 minutes, add watercress and wild onion and simmer for another 30 minutes over the campfire. If I have a piece of bacon or a small piece of porcupine, I usually let that simmer with the stew.

HOME RECIPES

WATERCRESS AND WATER CHESTNUT SALAD

2 bunches watercress	2 teaspoons sesame seed oil
8 fresh water chestnuts	½ teaspoon salt
1 teaspoon soy sauce	1 teaspoon sugar

Wash the watercress under running water and discard any discolored leaves. Wash the chestnuts, peel and cut into ¼-inch slices, then chop them very fine on a chopping board.

In a 2 to 3-quart saucepan bring 1½ quarts of water to a boil over high heat. Drop the watercress into the boiling water, remove from heat immediately and drain. Pat leaves dry with paper towels and chop finely with a sharp knife.

Combine in a large bowl the soy sauce, sesame seed oil, salt and sugar, and mix thoroughly. Add the watercress and chestnuts and toss well. Refrigerate for at least 2 hours before serving.

At the very last moment before serving toss lightly.

CREAMED WATERCRESS

5 cups water	¼ cup heavy cream
2 pounds watercress	1½ teaspoons salt
4 tablespoons butter	¼ teaspoon pepper
1 cup flour	2 hard-boiled eggs
2 cups milk	

Bring water to the boil in a 2-quart enamel or stainless steel saucepan, put in the cleaned watercress and cook for 15 minutes. If boiled too long, watercress gets stringy. Drain in a sieve thoroughly, then chop into small pieces and set to one side.

In a 2-quart saucepan melt butter over moderate heat. Remove from heat and stir in flour. Pour in milk and cream all at once, stirring constantly with a wire whisk. Place over low heat and stir until the sauce is smooth and thick. Season with salt and pepper, then add the chopped watercress and cook for another 4 to 5 minutes until the watercress is heated through.

Place on a warm serving dish, sprinkle the chopped hard-boiled eggs on top, and garnish with parsley. Smoked salmon goes well with this dish, and may be arranged around the edge of your serving dish.

STEWED WATERCRESS

4 tablespoons butter	½ teaspoon salt
4 tablespoons flour	¼ teaspoon white pepper
2 cups milk	2 pounds watercress
¼ cup heavy cream	

In a 2-quart stainless steel saucepan, melt butter over moderate heat. Remove from heat and stir in the flour. Pour the milk and cream in all at once and stirring constantly with a wire whisk, cook over low heat until the sauce is smooth and thick. Season with salt and pepper.

Parboil the watercress for 7 or 8 minutes, drain in a sieve, then chop very finely. Add to the sauce and heat through.

Serve with finely chopped watercress as garnish.

WATERCRESS PANCAKES

½ pound watercress	2 tablespoons butter, melted
1½ cups milk	2 eggs
1 teaspoon salt	½ teaspoon sugar
⅛ teaspoon nutmeg	1 to 2 tablespoons butter
1 cup flour	

Parboil the watercress for 7 or 8 minutes. Drain in a sieve, squeeze dry and chop finely. Set aside.

In a large mixing bowl, combine the milk, salt, nutmeg and flour, and then stir in the melted butter. In a separate bowl, combine the eggs and sugar and stir this into the batter. Gradually add the watercress.

With a paper towel, coat the bottom of a heavy skillet with about a teaspoon of soft butter and set over moderate heat. When the pan is very hot, drop 2 tablespoons of the batter onto the skillet and flatten to form a 4-inch disk.

Cook the pancakes 2 or 3 at a time for 3 to 4 minutes on each side, or until they have browned lightly. Keep warm on a heated platter.

Serve as a vegetable course.

WATERCRESS WITH PINE NUTS AND HAZELNUTS

¼ cup olive oil	1 pound watercress, finely
1 large garlic clove, cut lengthwise	chopped
¼ cup pine nuts	½ cup finely diced bacon
¼ cup finely chopped hazelnuts	1 teaspoon salt
	½ teaspoon pepper

In a heavy 12-inch skillet, heat the olive oil till a light haze forms above it. Add the garlic and cook for 2 minutes, stirring constantly. Remove with a slotted spoon and discard.

Add the pine and hazelnuts and cook for 5 to 6 minutes or until they are browned. Add bacon, salt and pepper, and cook for 2 to 3 minutes. Dry the watercress well before you add it to the hot oil, or it will splatter.

Working fast, toss the watercress in the mixture, making sure it is well coated and barely heated through. If you keep the watercress too long on the heat, it will lose some of its crispness.

Taste for seasoning and serve at once.

BAKED PIKE STUFFED WITH WATERCRESS AND WILD RICE

3-pound pike	½ cup parsley, finely chopped
1 cup wild rice	¼ cup leeks, finely chopped
2 cups watercress	1 tablespoon salt
½ cup wild onion, minced	3 tablespoons heavy cream
2 tablespoons butter	8 tablespoons soft butter
2 hard-boiled eggs, chopped	½ cup dry white wine

Clean and scale the pike. Remove the backbone but leave the head and tail on. Wash inside and out under cold running water and dry thoroughly with paper towels. Set aside.

In a heavy 3-quart saucepan, bring 2 quarts of water to a boil. Add ¼ teaspoon salt and pour in the wild rice in a slow stream so that the boiling never stops. Simmer for 20 minutes or until the rice is still slightly firm. Drain in a large sieve and place the sieve over the saucepan to dry.

In a small bowl toss the watercress with the onion. Melt the butter over high heat. When it gives off a nutty aroma, lower the heat and add the watercress and onion mixture. Cook for 5 minutes, then transfer to a large mixing bowl and add the chopped eggs, cooked rice, parsley and leeks. Season to taste and add the heavy cream. Mix thoroughly. Stuff the fish with this filling and close the opening by sewing together.

Preheat oven to 375°. In a baking dish melt the 8 tablespoons of butter over moderate heat. Place the fish on its side in the dish, raise the heat and cook the fish until it is golden brown (about 5 minutes). Turn the fish over and brown the other side.

Remove the fish, being careful not to break it apart, and drain the butter into a small bowl. Line the baking dish with a piece of aluminum foil and using a pastry brush and reserved butter, grease the foil. Tie a string from the snout of the fish around the tail so it will stand upright in a nice curve, and set it on the foil. Pour the wine into the bottom of the baking dish and place in the oven. Lower the heat to 350° and bake for 30 minutes, basting with a bulb baster every 5 minutes. When the fish is almost cooked, raise the heat for 5 minutes and let it bake until golden brown.

Remove from oven and carefully slide the foil with the fish onto a heated platter. Remove string and serve at once with melted butter in a separate dish as a complement.

WATERCRESS OMELET

1½ cups watercress, finely chopped	1 teaspoon lemon juice
2 tablespoons fresh white bread crumbs	¼ teaspoon salt
	½ teaspoon sugar
3 tablespoons milk	4 eggs
4 tablespoons grated cheese	2 tablespoons butter

Preheat the broiler for 5 minutes. In a 2-quart saucepan, bring 3 cups water and ¼ teaspoon salt to a brisk boil. Dump the watercress into the boiling water, remove from heat and drain in a large sieve.

In a large mixing bowl soak bread crumbs in the milk for a few minutes. Stir in watercress, grated cheese, lemon juice, salt and sugar. In another bowl beat the eggs with a whisk until they are blended, then stir them into the bread mixture.

In a large heavy skillet, melt the butter over high heat. When it gives off a nutty aroma, reduce heat and pour in the bread mixture. Cook over moderate heat for 4 minutes or until the eggs are firm but moist. Slide the skillet under the broiler for a minute to brown the top. Serve at once.

SAUTÉED WATERCRESS WITH CALVES' LIVER

4 tablespoons butter	½ teaspoon pepper
½ cup minced wild onions	2 tablespoons dry red wine
2 cups watercress, finely chopped	2 tablespoons parsley, finely
1 pound calves' liver	chopped
½ teaspoon salt	

Heat 2 tablespoons butter over high heat. When it gives off a nutty aroma, reduce heat, add the onions, and cook for 8 minutes. Then stir in the watercress and cook for another 4 minutes. Set aside.

In the meantime, cut the liver into ¼-inch strips crosswise. Pat the strips dry with paper towels and season with salt and pepper. Heat the rest of the butter over high heat in the same way as above, and drop in the liver to sauté, turning frequently. Cook until it is lightly browned, as it should be in about 3 minutes. Liver should be cooked for a very short time over high heat, as it has a tendency to get tough if cooked over low heat for a long time.

Stir in the watercress and onion and cook for another 3 minutes. Transfer liver and watercress to a heated platter.

Immediately pour wine into the skillet, boil briskly for 2 minutes, scraping in any browned bits clinging to pan. Stir in parsley and pour sauce over liver and watercress.

Serve at once.

WINTERGREEN

WINTERGREEN

(Gaultheria procumbens)

This is a low shrub, barely six inches high, found in rocky woods. The plant has creeping stems, half-hidden by foliage, from which grow reddish branches bearing ovate, glossy, leathery leaves. The leaves are serrated with bristle-tipped teeth and are gathered in a tuft at the top of the slender stalks, with the fleshy white or pinkish urn-shaped flowers nodding underneath. The fruits are bright scarlet, mealy but spicy in flavor.

This plant is aromatic in taste and is frequently eaten whole — foliage, berries and all. As a survival food it is important because the berries cling to the plant all winter. The spiciness is due to the volatile oil of Gaultheria which is a stimulant, astringent and diuretic. The generic name of the plant was given in honor of a Quebec physician Dr. Jean-François Gaultier, who discovered its medical properties. This plant is known by several local names, such as checkerberry, boxberry, spiceberry, partridgeberry, ground berry, mountain tea, and creeping snowberry. I believe the wintergreen is the best-known wild edible plant in North America. The western relative of this plant, *Gaultheria shallon,* is less spicy than the eastern plant, but the berries are still highly esteemed by the Indians, who call the plant salal.

IN THE BUSH

The berries can be eaten raw and have a refreshing taste, sweet and dry.

As Tea: When hunting or fishing in the fall, I usually pick a handful of leaves and put them in my pocket to be used as chewing gum or to make a cup of tea when I light a campfire. By tearing the leaves into small pieces, you provide even more flavor. If you are lucky enough to find a wild bee's nest and can steal some honey from it, you will have a drink that you won't forget.

In the olden days, the plant was collected in great quantities, dried and packed to be shipped to the nearest confectionary to be soaked in water and distilled. The familiar wintergreen flavor, so common in drugstores and markets, is no longer made from the plant but obtained synthetically.

WINTERGREEN PANCAKES

4 cups ripe wintergreen berries	3 cups milk
2 tablespoons sugar	1 cup flour
Juice of a lemon	6 tablespoons melted butter
3 eggs	½ teaspoon salt

Clean and rinse the berries under cold running water. Mix with sugar. Add the lemon juice. Crush the berries slightly and set in the refrigerator. Make this filling at least 2 hours before you intend to make the pancakes.

In a large mixing bowl beat the eggs together with ½ cup of milk for 3 to 4 minutes or until they are well mixed. Add the flour all at once and beat to a heavy, smooth, creamy consistency. Beat in the rest of the milk, the melted butter and the salt.

Place a 10-inch pancake skillet over high heat and, when a drop of water flicked on its surface bounces around, lower the heat to the next setting. Using a pastry brush, grease the skillet with a little melted butter. Because of the great amount of butter in the batter, no further greasing should be necessary.

Drop in a tablespoon of batter and tilt the skillet so that it will flow in a wide circle and the pancakes will be very thin. After 1 or 2 minutes or when the edges begin to brown, turn the pancake over and cook for another 2 minutes. Place the pancakes on a heated platter and keep warm in the oven. When all the batter is used, you should have 20 pancakes about 7 inches in diameter. Remove the pancakes from the oven, and place one at a time on a plate. Put 2 tablespoons of the crushed wintergreen berries at one side of the pancake and roll it up. Place the rolled pancakes on a hot serving platter side by side and sprinkle a little sugar on top of each. Serve hot.

WINTERGREEN BERRY JELLY

2 quarts wintergreen berries	2 pectin enzyme tablets (can be
3 cups water	obtained from Wine-Art stores)
2 cups sugar or more	

Clean the berries and wash under running water, removing stems. Drop into a large soup kettle, add the water and bring to a boil over high heat. Reduce the heat and cook for 45 minutes, stirring occasionally.

Set a large sieve atop a large pot and line with a double layer of dampened cheesecloth. Pour the wintergreen berries into the sieve. Allow the juice to drain into the pot without disturbing it. Squeezing the cheesecloth will make the jelly cloudy.

After the juice has drained thoroughly, measure it and return it to the pot. Discard the berries. Add 1 cup of sugar for each cup of juice. Add the pectin enzyme tablets, well broken up, and bring to a boil over high heat, stirring until the sugar has dissolved. Boil uncovered until the jelly reaches the temperature of 220° on a candy thermometer.

Remove the pot from the heat and carefully skim off the surface foam. Ladle the jelly into hot sterilized jars or jelly glasses. When cool seal with wax.

WINTERGREEN BERRY PIE

4 eggs	1½ cups wintergreen berries
2 cups maple syrup	Pie shell
2 tablespoons butter, melted	

With a rotary beater beat the eggs in a mixing bowl for ½ minute. Slowly pour in the maple syrup and continue to beat until they are well combined. With a wire whisk beat in the melted butter, then stir in the wintergreen berries. Put in the refrigerator.

PIE SHELL

1¼ cups all purpose flour	⅛ teaspoon salt
4 tablespoons lard	3 tablespoons ice water
2 tablespoons butter	

Preheat the oven to 425°. Using a large mixing bowl, mix the flour, lard, butter and salt. Using your fingertips, rub the flour and fat together until they are like coarse meal. Pour the ice water over the mixture, toss together, and press and knead gently until the dough can be gathered into a compact ball. Dust with flour, wrap in a piece of wax paper and chill for 1 hour.

Butter a 9-inch pie plate. On the floured surface of a baking board roll the dough out into a circle about ⅛ inch thick and 13 to 14 inches in diameter. Lift it up on the rolling pin and unroll it over the pie plate. Leave enough slack in the middle of the pastry to enable you to line the plate without pulling the dough.

Trim the pastry to within ½ inch of the rim of the pie plate and fold the extra ½ inch under to make a double thickness all around the rim. With your fingers press the pastry down around the rim. To prevent the unfilled pie shell from buckling, line the inside of the piecrust with a sheet of lightly buttered foil.

Bake the shell in the middle of the oven for 8 minutes. Remove the foil and let the shell cool.

Carefully pour the filling into the pie shell. Bake the pie in the middle of the oven for 35 to 40 minutes, or until the filling is firm. This pie is best served cold.

GRIDDLECAKES WITH WINTERGREEN BERRIES

2 cups all purpose flour	2 cups milk
2 teaspoons baking powder	¼ cup melted butter
1 cup sugar	2 cups wintergreen berries
1 teaspoon salt	¼ cup vegetable oil
3 eggs, lightly beaten	

Sift the flour, baking powder, sugar and salt together into a large mixing bowl. Make a hole in the middle of the flour mixture and pour in the milk and eggs. Using a large wooden spoon, mix together only long enough to blend, then stir in the butter. Do not overmix. Fold the wintergreen berries into the batter.

Heat a griddle over moderate heat until a drop of water will dance on the surface and evaporate almost immediately.

Grease the griddle very lightly with a pastry brush dipped in the oil. Pour the batter from a pitcher into the hot pan to form pancakes about 3 inches in diameter. Cook for 4 minutes on one side and with a metal spatula turn and cook for about 2 minutes or until the pancake is golden brown.

Stack the pancakes on a heated platter and serve with maple syrup.

WINTERGREEN TEA

Wintergreen leaves make an excellent tea. I usually collect as many leaves as possible in the late fall. The pre-drying procedure is started by spreading them out on a bed of newspapers when I come home from the bush. After a couple of days of drying in the sun, (I carefully take them inside during the night) they are ready to be cut into smaller pieces. Put the leaves on a baking sheet with upturned sides, and leave overnight in a 200° oven. In the morning, spread the leaves on a piece of paper to cool. At this time your house will have an aroma of wintergreen which is most delightful.

Place the shredded leaves in plastic freezer bags and close the bags carefully. Put the bags into sealers and seal the lid carefully with wax.

When you are making tea, warm the teapot for 5 minutes while the kettle comes to the boil. Pour out the warming water and place a tablespoon of wintergreen leaves in the bottom of the pot. Pour boiling water over the leaves and let steep for 5 minutes before serving. Serves 6.

WOOD SORREL

WOOD SORREL

(Oxalis acetosella, Oxalis violacea)

Wood sorrel is a small delicate plant about 7 inches in height, with a sour juice. Its stems are round, slender and easily bruised. Light green clover-shaped leaves grow on the end of each stem. The roots are bulbous. Its flowers are five-petaled and yellow *(Oxalis acetosella)* or purple *(Oxalis violacea)* in color. The plant with purple flowers is more common.

Wood sorrel is also called sour grass, sour trefoil and shamrock. It clusters in shady places in damp woods. I have seen this little plant covering acres as thickly as grass.

This plant should not be eaten in large quantity at one time because of its high concentration of "salt of lemons" or oxalic acid, which is a poison. However, a moderate use is no health hazard.

Eskimos and Laplanders, who ferment the wood sorrel leaves and use them as a sauerkraut, seemingly know the danger of eating too much or too often of this plant. I remember one time travelling with a band of Laplanders when this dish was served. I liked it so much I wanted a refill but was refused — an action very uncommon among people who will share their last bit of food with you. When I asked the reason for this strange, hostile attitude, I was told that if I ate too much, the white wolf in the sky would overtake and kill me by thirst, tied to a dwarf birch in the wilderness.

IN THE BUSH

As a Vegetable: This plant is an excellent "pepper upper" or thirst quencher when the stems and leaves are eaten raw. And they are a superb addition to any salad. The onion-like tubers may be eaten raw or boiled.

As a Beverage: This plant makes an excellent substitute for lemonade if boiled in water for about 15 minutes and cooled. Serve with sugar added. The Indians used wood sorrel for a sort of lemonade in which they mixed wild bee honey — a most·appealing drink.

As an Herb: An Indian I once travelled with made an excellent stew of porcupine and a couple of handfuls of wood sorrel leaves seasoned with a pinch of coltsfoot salt. It was delicious.

As a Condiment: A pickle of the tuberous roots and a handful of red ants soaked in water overnight can be made and is very tasty when served with small game which has been cooked in the same pot as the ants and the wood sorrel roots.

HOME RECIPES

BAKED PIKE STUFFED WITH WOOD SORREL LEAVES AND TUBERS

1 cup wood sorrel leaves	3 to 4-pound pike
½ cup wood sorrel tubers	1 tablespoon salt
4 tablespoons butter	½ teaspoon pepper
4 tablespoons heavy cream	4 tablespoons butter
½ cup dry bread crumbs	1 cup dry white wine
½ teaspoon salt	

Wash and clean the wood sorrel leaves and tubers. Dry the leaves on paper towels and shred them. Chop the tubers finely.

Place a 10-inch heavy stainless steel skillet over high heat and melt 4 tablespoons of butter. When it gives off a nutty odor, add the leaves and tubers. Cook for 5 minutes, making sure all the greens are well coated with butter. Transfer to a large mixing bowl. Add the heavy cream, bread crumbs and salt. Mix the ingredients well and set aside.

Clean and scale the pike, leaving on the head and tail. Wash under running water and pat dry with paper towels. Rub the cavity of the fish with the salt and pepper, and fill with the wood sorrel stuffing. Close the opening with small skewers, and crisscross kitchen string around them.

Preheat the oven to 400°. Using a baking dish large enough to hold the fish comfortably, melt the rest of the butter over moderate heat. Place the fish in the baking dish, and cook in the oven for about 5 minutes, using a bulb baster to baste it. Carefully turn the fish over to its other side and repeat the operation. When the fish is golden brown on all sides, lower the heat to 350° and add the wine. Bake uncovered in the middle of the oven for 35 minutes.

Serve the fish direct from the baking dish accompanied by a bowl of hot clarified butter.

SOUR WOOD SORREL SAUCE

2 tablespoons butter	1 tablespoon white vinegar
¼ cup wild onions, finely chopped	½ cup wood sorrel leaves and
½ cup flour	tubers, finely chopped
1½ cups beef stock	½ cup heavy cream
1 tablespoon sugar	

In a heavy stainless steel saucepan, melt the butter over high heat. When it gives off a nutty odor, lower the heat and add the finely chopped onions. Cook for 5 minutes or until they are lightly browned, then add the flour and cook, stirring constantly, until the mixture is lightly browned.

Add the stock, sugar, vinegar and bring to a boil. Simmer over moderate heat for about 15 minutes, or until the sauce is smooth and creamy. Pour through a sieve, pressing down lightly on the onions to retrieve as much flavor as possible. Return to the saucepan, add the wood sorrel leaves and tubers, stir in the cream, and simmer until hot. Taste for seasoning.

Serve in a sauceboat with boiled beef.

WOOD SORREL AND SOUR CREAM DRESSING

2 cups wood sorrel leaves, finely chopped
1 cup water
1 cup sour cream

2 teaspoons sugar
1 teaspoon salt
½ teaspoon pepper

Clean and wash the wood sorrel leaves under running water. Place a heavy stainless steel saucepan over high heat, add water and bring to a boil. Add the 2 cups wood sorrel leaves and cook for 5 minutes. Remove the pan from the heat and let steep on the side of the fire for 2 hours.

Pour the sour cream into a large mixing bowl. With a wooden spoon, stir in the sugar, salt, pepper and 4 tablespoons of the cooled wood sorrel juice.

Beat with an electric beater until the dressing is smooth and thoroughly blended. Taste for seasoning — it may need more wood sorrel juice.

I use this dressing on many of my wild salads.

WOOD SORREL CLARET CUP

2 cups wood sorrel tubers
1 cup water
1 ounce sugar
1 tablespoon angostura bitters
1 liqueur glass brandy
1 liqueur glass maraschino

1 liqueur glass curaçao
1 cup water
1½ bottles red wine
26 ounces soda water
5 sprigs mint

Clean and wash the wood sorrel tubers. Chop them finely. Over high heat bring water to a boil and add the tubers. Boil for 5 minutes. Remove from heat and cool, then strain through a fine sieve. You should have about 1 cup of fluid.

Pour the liquid into a glass bowl, add the sugar, angostura bitters, brandy, maraschino, curaçao, red wine and soda water.

Cover and let the whole mixture infuse for 1½ hours in the refrigerator. Strain through a fine sieve. Add a few pieces of ice and the mint.

Serve cold in chilled lemonade glasses.

YELLOW CLOVER

YELLOW CLOVER
(Trifolium agrarium)

Everyone who has searched for the lucky four leaf clover knows this plant. As a general rule it is sprawling. The leaves are a soft light green and grow in groups of three. The flowers are bright yellow and grow in clusters.

Clover is a good source of the honey bee's all-important nectar. It is interesting that when clover first was introduced to Australia, it failed to reproduce itself until the bumblebee also was brought in. The green and the flower are both edible and require only a good washing in running water. As a boy, I remember picking up the flower and eating it raw. Eaten this way, you really notice the sweet honey taste.

IN THE BUSH

As a Fresh Vegetable: It is a very common practice among the Indians to eat the flowers, stems and seeds after they have been cleaned and dipped in salted water.

As a Cooked Vegetable: Melt some porcupine fat or bacon fat in the frying pan until it is very hot. Cut the clover into small pieces and cook in the fat. Remove from the pan and drip dry on a piece of birch bark. Let it cool before eating.

HOME RECIPES
CLOVER OMELET

3 strips bacon	3 tablespoons water
2 cups clover flowers, stems and seeds	Salt and pepper
3 eggs	2 tablespoons butter

Chop the bacon into small pieces and place in a frying pan. Clean and rinse the clover and chop finely. When the bacon turns crisp, add the clover and fry for 5 minutes, stirring constantly.

In a bowl combine the eggs, the water, and a little bit of salt and pepper and beat until you have a fluffy consistency. Heat the butter in an omelet pan until it gives off a nutty smell. This will not only improve the taste but also will ensure the perfect heat for the setting of the eggs.

Pour in the beaten and seasoned eggs, and stir briskly with a fork in order to heat the whole mass evenly.

When the omelet is cooked, take the filling and put it on the omelet and briskly roll it up and transfer to a serving platter. When the omelet is on the platter, a piece of butter may be quickly drawn across its surface to make it glossy.

CLOVER SOUP

2 cups clover flowers and leaves	3 medium-sized potatoes
1 medium onion	Salt and pepper
4 tablespoons butter	Parsley
2 pints water	Grated cheese

Cut the clover leaves and flowers into small pieces; mince the onion. Stew them in butter together in a large saucepan. When they are soft, add 2 pints of water. Peel and quarter the potatoes and add them with the necessary salt and pepper. Cook gently for 20 minutes.

Drain the cooking liquor and save it. Mash the potatoes, dilute the purée with the cooking liquor and rub through a fine sieve. Bring to a boil and simmer 2 minutes. Garnish with finely chopped parsley and sprinkle with the cheese.

CLOVER CARAMEL CUSTARD

3 cups yellow clover flowers	¾ cup sugar
1½ cups milk	6 egg yolks
1½ cups heavy cream	2 tablespoons rum

Preheat the oven to 350°. In a heavy 1 to 1½-quart saucepan, heat ½ quart water until it boils. Add the cleaned and washed clover blossoms and simmer for 5 minutes. Drain the blossoms in a colander and set aside. Clean the saucepan and add the milk and heavy cream. Place over moderate heat until small bubbles appear around the edges of the pan. Do not let boil. Set aside.

In an 8-inch heavy skillet, caramelize the sugar over low heat until it melts and turns a light golden brown. Be careful not to burn the sugar. Pour the heated milk and cream into the sugar in a thin stream, stirring constantly with a large wooden spoon. Stir until the caramel has completely dissolved.

With an electric beater beat the egg yolks in a large bowl until they are well blended. Slowly pour the cream mixture into the eggs, constantly stirring with the wooden spoon. When well mixed, add the drained yellow clover blossoms and stir well. Stir in the rum and blend thoroughly.

Pour the mixture into 12 4-ounce custard cups. Place the cups in a large roasting pan and pour in enough boiling water to come halfway up the sides of the cups. Bake for 45 minutes or until a knife inserted in the center of the custard comes out clean and dry. Cool at room temperature, then refrigerate for at least 4 hours. To unmold the custard, dip the cup in hot water for a second and turn a chilled serving plate upside down on the custard cup. Holding on to both the plate and the custard cup, quickly invert them.

DEEP-FRIED CLOVER BLOSSOM FRITTERS

1 cup flour	¼ cup dark rum
½ teaspoon salt	½ cup sugar
1 egg, lightly beaten	3 cups yellow clover blossoms,
1 tablespoon butter, melted	washed and cleaned
1 cup milk	Vegetable oil
1 egg white	Confectioners' sugar

Sift ½ cup flour and the salt into a large mixing bowl. Stir in the beaten egg and the melted butter and then the milk. Stir until the batter is smooth. Set aside and let rest for 1 hour at room temperature. Beat the egg white with a rotary beater until stiff, and fold into the batter just before you are ready to use it.

Combine the rum and sugar in a mixing bowl. Stir until the sugar is dissolved. Drop the clover blossoms into the rum mixture and stir to make sure they are well coated. Set aside for 30 minutes, stirring occasionally.

Heat the vegetable oil in a deep fat fryer or a large heavy skillet until it reaches 375° on a deep-frying thermometer. Place the soaked clover blossoms on a double layer of paper towels. Dip them into the remaining ½ cup flour and shake away the excess. With tongs, dip them in the batter, then deep-fry them for 3 to 4 minutes, 7 or 8 at a time. When golden brown on all sides, transfer the fritters to paper towels to drain while you fry the remaining blossoms. Serve warm, sprinkled with confectioners' sugar if you wish.

CLOVER AND WINE LEMONADE

6 cups yellow clover blossoms	1 bottle dry red wine
and young leaves	1 bottle dry white wine
1 lemon	½ cup sugar

Clean the blossoms and leaves well. Discard any wilted or black leaves. Chop finely. Remove the yellow peel from the lemon, being careful not to cut into the white pith. Set aside. Squeeze the juice from the lemon and pour into a 3 to 4-quart serving pitcher. Add the chopped yellow clover blossoms and leaves. Pour in the wine. Cut the lemon peel in ½-inch strips and add it. Stir with a long-handled wooden spoon until well mixed.

Refrigerate for at least 48 hours, stirring occasionally. Drain the mixture through a large sieve over a large mixing bowl. Retrieve the yellow lemon peelings and discard the clover blossoms and leaves.

Clean the serving pitcher and replace the drained mixture. Add sugar and taste for sweetness. Add more sugar if desired. Stir well to dissolve sugar. Serve in frosted wine glasses filled with crushed ice and garnish with the lemon peel.

PORK CHOPS BAKED WITH YELLOW CLOVER

10 cups yellow clover blossoms	6 pork chops, ¾ inch thick
4 tablespoons butter	Salt and pepper
½ cup wild onion, minced	1 cup milk
½ teaspoon salt	1 cup heavy cream
¼ teaspoon pepper	1 cup dry red wine
3 tablespoons butter	2 tablespoons dry bread crumbs

Clean and wash the clover blossoms well. Discard all darkened or wilted flowers. In a soup kettle, bring 4 quarts water to a boil over high heat. Drop in the washed clover flowers and boil for 8 minutes. Take the kettle off the heat, drain through a large sieve, and place the boiled clover blossoms on a double thickness of paper towels.

In a heavy 12-inch skillet, melt the 4 tablespoons butter over high heat. When it gives off a nutty odor, reduce the heat and add the onions. Cook for 5 or 6 minutes until golden brown. Stir in the clover blossoms, salt and pepper. Cook for 10 minutes. Transfer the contents of the skillet to a large mixing bowl and set aside.

Melt 3 tablespoons of butter in the skillet over high heat and when the foam subsides, season the pork chops with salt and pepper. Put them in the skillet to brown for 4 minutes. Turn them over and brown on the other side.

Remove the chops from the skillet, pour in the milk and heat it to the boiling point. Scrape all the bits and pieces left from the chops into the milk and add the heavy cream and the red wine. Simmer over very low heat.

Preheat the oven to 375°. Grease a heavy, flameproof casserole with butter and spread a layer of the clover blossoms on the bottom. Cover with 3 pork chops and another layer of clover blossoms. Cover this layer with the 3 remaining pork chops. Finish with a layer of clover blossoms on top. Pour the wine and the cream mixture over top and place the casserole in the oven. Cook for 1 hour. Sprinkle the top with the bread crumbs and bake for another 30 minutes or until the top is browned and crusty. Serve from the casserole.

BRAISED YELLOW CLOVER BLOSSOMS

4 cups yellow clover blossoms	4 tablespoons honey
4 tablespoons butter	2 cups beef stock

Carefully clean the clover blossoms and discard any black or withered flowers. Wash under cold running water. In a 3-quart saucepan, bring 2 quarts salted water to a boil. Drop the clover blossoms in and cook for 8 minutes. Drain through a large sieve and set aside.

In a 12-inch skillet, melt the butter over high heat. When it gives off a nutty odor, reduce the heat and stir in the honey. Dissolve all the honey in the butter and add ½ cup of beef stock. Mix well over low heat. Add the clover blossoms and stir gently, making sure the blossoms are well covered on all sides. Preheat the oven to 350°.

In a well-greased, shallow flameproof casserole, put the clover blossoms from the skillet and add the rest of the beef stock. Boil on the top of the stove for 20 minutes. Cover the casserole with aluminum foil and place in the middle of the oven. In 20 minutes the stock should almost have cooked away and the clover blossoms should be slightly browned. Stir very gently to bring the moist bottom layer on top in the casserole, and serve at once.

YELLOW CLOVER SALAD

6 cups clover blossoms and leaves	¼ teaspoon black pepper
3 tablespoons olive oil	½ teaspoon dry mustard
1 tablespoon dry white wine	3 medium tomatoes
1 tablespoon white vinegar	½ cup wild onion
½ teaspoon salt	

Rinse and clean the young clover leaves, discarding all wilted and black leaves. Clean the blossoms, discarding any dark ones. Rinse and dry on paper towels.

To make the dressing: In a large mixing bowl, combine the oil, wine, vinegar, salt, pepper and the mustard. Beat them together with a spoon or whisk.

Cut the tomatoes in half, remove all the seeds, then cut the pulp into ¼-inch squares. Chop the onions finely. Chop the clover blossoms and leaves very finely. Add the onions, tomatoes and the clover blossoms to the bowl and toss with a large wooden spoon to coat the greens evenly with the dressing. Chill well in refrigerator. Transfer to a salad or serving bowl and stir again before serving.

ARROWHEAD

ARROWHEAD
(Sagittaria latifolia)

This plant grows in shallow water and gets its name from the shape of the leaves. The leaves are placed on erect stems, from 4 to 12 inches long, thrust directly up from the roots. The flowers are white, three-petaled and fragile, and usually appear in groups near the top of a naked spire that sometimes extends 1 foot above the leaves.

Indians from coast to coast on this continent used the arrowhead roots for food, usually boiling them or roasting them in hot coals in the campfire. The arrowhead roots are one of the most valuable native foods we have, as they are both nutritious and delectable. Today fishermen often cast their lures alongside beds of arrowhead in order to catch lurking bass or pike. However, it is not often recognized as food, and many a man has died of hunger within easy reach of this valuable edible plant without knowing how close he was to salvation.

The arrowhead has many names. The California Chinese call it tule potato, the Indians call it wapato and katniss, other names are duck potato or swan potato. An old Swedish saying is "A cherished child has many names."

The small tubers look much like new potatoes and vary in size from a egg to BB shot. They mature after midsummer, but you can use them all winter if you can get to them. To harvest them do as the Indians did, using their toes to dislodge the tubers, which will float up to the surface after they have been loosened. Or use the more modern method of digging with a hoe. In a short time you can loosen more tubers than you can eat in a day.

IN THE BUSH

As a Raw Vegetable: The tubers can be eaten raw with salt, but they taste better cooked.

As a Cooked Vegetable: I like them wrapped in green leaves and put into the coals of the campfire, where I leave them for 1 hour to roast. I usually put as many as I can into the fire, and what I don't eat immediately I later make into a salad.

As a Salad: The salad is easy to prepare. Peel the tubers and slice them in ¼-inch slices. Put them into a bowl or a cup made out of birch bark.

Mix with wild honey and wild leeks which have been finely chopped. If I have any fat, I usually put some into the mixture.

HOME RECIPES

ARROWHEAD ROOT PANCAKES

10 egg-sized arrowhead tubers	**¼ cup milk**
Juice of 2 lemons	**½ teaspoon caraway seeds, crushed**
½ cup flour	**4 tablespoons bacon fat**
½ teaspoon salt	

Peel the arrowhead tubers and, to prevent discoloring, drop them into a bowl of cold water into which the lemon juice has been squeezed. Try to peel the tubers as thinly as possible.

In a large mixing bowl combine the flour, salt, milk and caraway seeds. Stir well. One at a time, take the arrowhead tubers and grate them finely. Put into a sieve and press hard to get as much water out of them as possible. Stir the tubers into the flour and milk mixture.

In a heavy 10 to 12-inch skillet melt the bacon fat over moderate heat. Pour in 1 tablespoon of batter for each pancake. You can easily cook 5 to 6 pancakes at a time, making sure that you are leaving enough space around so they can spread.

Fry the pancakes for 5 to 6 minutes on each side, or until they are golden brown and crisp around the edges. Transfer to a heated platter, cover with foil, and put into a 125° oven to keep warm.

Serve the pancakes as soon as they are ready, accompanied, if you wish, with cranberry jelly.

ARROWHEAD TUBERS WITH ANCHOVY

14 egg-sized arrowhead tubers	**½ teaspoon pepper**
Juice of 2 lemons	**4 tablespoons dry bread crumbs**
3 tablespoons butter	**½ cup milk**
4 wild onions, thinly sliced	**½ cup heavy cream**
20 flat anchovy fillets	**6 whole peppercorns**

Preheat the oven to 425°. Clean and scrape the arrowhead tubers. Peel very thinly and cut them into strips ¼ inch thick and as long as possible. Place the strips in a bowl with water and the lemon juice to keep the tubers from discoloring.

In a 10-inch skillet melt 1 tablespoon of the butter and place over high heat. When it gives off a nutty aroma, place the sliced wild onions in the pan and fry until they are golden but not brown.

Butter a 2-quart fireproof casserole, making sure the sides are well greased. Drain the arrowhead tubers in a sieve and put them on a double thickness of paper towels to dry completely.

Arrange a layer of arrowhead strips on the bottom of the casserole and alternate the layers with onions and anchovies, making sure you end with a layer of arrowhead tubers. Sprinkle each layer with a little pepper. Spread the bread crumbs evenly over the top. Cut 2 tablespoons of butter into squares and put on top. Pour the milk and cream over the casserole and add the whole peppercorns on top. Bake in the center of the oven for 1 hour or until the arrowhead tubers are tender when pierced with the tip of a sharp knife and the liquid is all gone. If necessary, cover the casserole with aluminum foil after the top has browned.

CARAMELIZED ARROWHEAD TUBERS

25 egg-sized arrowhead tubers   8 tablespoons butter
½ cup sugar

Scrape and clean the arrowhead tubers. Put them unpeeled into a pan of boiling water with a little salt and cook for 25 minutes or until they are soft when pierced with a toothpick.

Peel the arrowhead tubers, making sure you do not remove more of the skin than is necessary.

Melt the sugar in a 12-inch heavy skillet over low heat. Cook very slowly to ensure that it will not burn — when it has taken on a golden brown color it will not take very long for it to burn. Stir in the butter well before you add the arrowhead tubers. Make sure that you do not crowd the pan. Shake it and let the tubers roll freely so they will be coated on all sides with the caramel. Remove the caramelized tubers to a heated serving bowl and keep hot until all the arrowhead tubers are coated.

This dish is to be served as hot as possible.

ARROWHEAD TUBERS IN PARSLEY SAUCE

12 egg-sized arrowhead tubers   1½ cups boiling water
  Juice of 2 lemons   2 tablespoons finely chopped
½ cup finely chopped wild onions   parsley
¼ teaspoon pepper   5 tablespoons flour
1 teaspoon salt   2 tablespoons heavy cream
1 teaspoon minced garlic

Brush and clean the arrowhead tubers and peel them as thinly as you can. Slice crosswise into ½-inch rounds and drop into a bowl of water into which the juice of the lemons has been squeezed.

Using a heavy skillet, heat the butter over a high heat until it gives off a nutty aroma. Add the arrowhead tubers and turn them frequently with a metal spatula until they are golden brown on all sides.

Scatter the onions, pepper and the garlic on top of the arrowhead tubers. Pour in the water and add the parsley. Do not stir but gently shake the skillet back and forth.

Cover the skillet tightly and simmer over low heat for at least 35 minutes or until the arrowhead tubers are tender but not falling apart. Shake the skillet occasionally to prevent the tubers from sticking.

Remove the tubers with a slotted spatula, trying to leave as much of the onion and parsley in the pan as possible.

Add the flour and constantly stir the mixture until it is smooth. It may be necessary to add the tablespoons of heavy cream to get the right creamy consistency. Add salt and pepper to taste.

Pour the sauce over the arrowhead tubers and serve hot with a sprinkle of freshly chopped parsley on top.

ARROWHEAD ROOTS WITH SALT PICKEREL AND ONIONS

2 pounds salt pickerel fillets	½ cup finely chopped chives
Coarse salt	1 cup heavy cream
12 egg-sized arrowhead tubers	5 hard-cooked eggs
4 tablespoons butter	2 tablespoons parsley
4 wild onions	

Start a week ahead. Put the fillets of pickerel in a glass, enamel or stainless steel bowl in layers with coarse salt in between. After a week, take the fish out of the brine and let stand overnight in a bowl of cold water.

Preheat the oven to 250°. Coat the sides and bottom of an 8-inch casserole with butter.

Drop the arrowhead tubers into a 2-quart saucepan and add water to cover. Bring to a boil and cook for 20 minutes. Drain, peel the tubers and cut into ¼-inch slices. Set aside.

Drain the pickerel fillets, rinse under cold water, place in a saucepan, and add fresh water to cover. Bring to a boil over high heat, reduce the heat, and simmer for 10 minutes.

Drain thoroughly. Separate the fish into coarse flakes and remove any bones. Set aside.

Cut the onion crosswise into ¼-inch slices and separate into rings. In a heavy 12-inch skillet heat the butter until it gives off a nutty aroma. Add the onion rings, stirring frequently, and cook for 8 minutes or until soft but not brown. Stir in the chopped chives and cook for 5 minutes over low heat.

Spread half the arrowhead tubers in the bottom of the casserole, cover them with half the pickerel, and repeat the layers with the rest of the arrowhead tubers and fish and onions. Pour the cream over top.

Bake in the middle of the oven for 30 minutes. Garnish with ¼-inch slices of the hard-cooked eggs, cut crosswise, and sprinkle with chopped parsley.

ARROWHEAD ROOT BALLS FILLED WITH BACON

21 egg-sized arrowhead tubers	1 cup flour
Juice of 2 lemons	1 teaspoon salt
10 slices bacon	2 dozen whole allspice
1 egg	2 wild onions, minced

Put 6 egg-sized arrowhead tubers in a 2-quart saucepan, fill with water, add a little salt. Bring to a boil, turn the heat down and simmer for 25 minutes. Take the pan off the heat and drain. Peel the tubers and set aside.

Clean and brush the remaining tubers. Peel them as thinly as possible. As you peel put them in a pot of water into which you have squeezed the lemon juice. Set aside.

Take the bacon and cut it lengthwise in ¼-inch strings then cut it in ¼-inch cubes crosswise. Put a 10-inch skillet over high heat, add the bacon, reduce the heat and fry for 5 minutes or until the bacon is crisp and golden brown. Set aside.

In a bowl mix the egg, flour, salt and allspice. Mash the boiled arrowhead tubers, using a little butter and milk, and add to the bowl. Grate the raw arrowhead tubers and add, mixing very well to make sure the mixture is smooth and soft.

Remove the bacon from the skillet and, with the bacon fat remaining, put the skillet over high heat until the fat starts smoking. Lower the heat and add the finely chopped onions. Fry until soft and transparent, but not brown. Remove with a slotted spoon and drain on a double layer of paper towels. When well drained, mix the onions with the bacon. Fill a 3 to 4-quart saucepan with 2½ quarts water, place on high heat, add 1 teaspoon salt and bring to a boil.

Form your arrowhead mixture into balls in your hands. Make a hole in the ball and put in the bacon filling. Close the hole and drop the ball into the boiling water. Cook in the water for 45 minutes. This dish is served with a white sauce with bacon crumbled into it.

ARROWHEAD PANCAKES

12 arrowhead tubers	1 teaspoon salt
Juice of 2 lemons	1 cup flour
1 egg	4 tablespoons butter

Scrape and clean the arrowhead tubers, rinse under cold running water, and peel as thinly as possible. Put the peeled tubers in a mixing bowl with water to which the lemon juice has been added. This is to prevent the tubers from discoloring.

In a mixing bowl beat the egg and salt until fluffy. Grate the arrowhead tubers and make sure all the fluid is added to the bowl. Stir in the flour a little at a time, making sure all the lumps are worked out. The batter will be thin.

In a 12-inch skillet melt the butter over high heat until it gives off a nutty aroma. Lower the heat to medium and with a spoon add the batter, making sure it is spread thinly. Fry for 2 minutes on one side, turn over and fry for another minute on the other side or until the edges turn golden brown. Serve with butter and maple syrup, and golden fried bacon.

SAILORS' STEW WITH ARROWHEAD TUBERS

15 arrowhead tubers	1 teaspoon salt
Juice of 2 lemons	1 teaspoon pepper
3 tablespoons butter	2 cups water
3 wild onions, sliced	1 cup beer or ale
3 pounds stewing beef	

Preheat oven to 350°. Scrape and clean the arrowhead tubers and peel the skin off as thinly as possible. Drop the peeled tubers into a bowl of water to which the lemon juice has been added. This is to prevent the tubers from discoloring.

Put a heavy 12-inch skillet over high heat and melt the butter in it. When it gives off a nutty aroma, lower the heat, add the sliced onions and brown them slightly. Remove the onions with a slotted spoon and set aside. Pound the meat thoroughly with a meat hammer to make it tender.

Put the meat in the skillet with the fat and increase the heat. Turn the meat so it will brown on all sides.

In a 2 or 3-quart casserole, place alternate layers of arrowhead tubers, meat and onions, making the bottom and top layers of tubers. Sprinkle the salt and pepper between the layers.

Put the water into the skillet and whisk out all the brown bits. Pour over the casserole and add the beer. Set the casserole in the oven and cook for 2 hours. Make sure the casserole is well covered and that the cooking fluid is not disappearing too fast. The stew is ready when all the liquid has disappeared.

CHOCOLATE ARROWHEAD TUBER CAKE

12 - 15 arrowhead tubers	1 teaspoon cinnamon
1 cup shortening	1 teaspoon cloves
2 cups sugar	½ teaspoon allspice
4 eggs	1 cup milk
2½ cups flour	1 teaspoon vanilla
1½ teaspoons baking powder	1 teaspoon lemon juice
1 teaspoon soda	1 cup raisins
1 teaspoon nutmeg	½ cup cocoa

Preheat the oven to 375°.

In a heavy 3 to 4-quart saucepan put 12 to 15 cleaned and scraped arrowhead tubers. Add water and bring to a boil. Lower the temperature and let the tubers cook for 35 to 40 minutes or until they are tender. Drain off the water and let the tubers cool to room temperature.

In a large mixing bowl cream the shortening and sugar with an electric beater. Peel the arrowhead tubers and mash them in the saucepan they were cooked in. Measure 1 cup and add to the mixture together with the eggs.

On a baking board sift together the flour, baking powder, soda and all the spices. Add the dried ingredients and the milk alternately to the creamed mixture and mix well with the electric beater on slow speed. Add the vanilla, lemon juice, raisins and cocoa. Blend well.

Put the mixture into a 10-inch cake pan, set in the middle of the oven and bake for 25 to 30 minutes. Serve without icing.

MY FAVORITE ARROWHEAD TUBER CASSEROLE

10 - 12 egg-sized arrowhead tubers	2 4-ounce cans sweetened
2 pimentos	evaporated milk
½ green pepper	½ cup old cheese
6 tablespoons butter	Salt and pepper
3 tablespoons flour	Cracker crumbs for topping

Place the arrowhead tubers in a 3 to 4-quart saucepan, add water to cover and a teaspoon of salt, and bring to the boil. Lower the temperature and cook covered for 35 to 40 minutes or until the tubers give no resistance when pierced with the tip of a sharp knife. Preheat the oven to 300°. Drain the tubers and when cool, peel and dice very thin. Grease a 2-quart casserole with 1 tablespoon butter on the bottom and sides. Half fill it with the diced arrowhead tubers and sprinkle cut pimento over top.

In a 10-inch skillet placed over high heat melt the remaining butter, and when it gives off a nutty aroma lower the heat and add the minced green pepper, the flour and the canned milk. Stir constantly, making sure all the ingredients are well mixed. Cook for 10 minutes. When the mixture has thickened, add the cheese and the salt and pepper to taste.

Pour the mixture over the arrowhead tubers but do not stir. Cover the casserole with cracker crumbs and dot butter on top. Put in the middle of the oven and bake for 1 hour. Make sure the mixture does not boil at any time.

ARROWHEAD PANCAKES WITH CHIVES

8 egg-sized arrowhead tubers	1 teaspoon pepper
Juice of 2 lemons	3 tablespoons butter
3 tablespoons chopped chives	2 tablespoons vegetable oil
2 teaspoons salt	

Peel the arrowhead tubers, making sure the skins taken off are as thin as possible. Drop the tubers into a mixing bowl with water to which the lemon juice has been added.

Grate the tubers coarsely over a mixing bowl so that the juices don't get lost. Try to work as fast as possible to prevent discoloration of the tubers. Mix into the grated arrowhead tubers the finely chopped chives, the salt and pepper.

Put a heavy 12-inch skillet over high heat and melt the butter. Gently mix the oil into the butter and lower the heat. The butter-oil mixture must be very hot but not so hot that it smokes. In floured hands make pancakes of 2 tablespoons of mix, flattening them out to about ¼ inch thick. Using a slotted metal spatula, add them to the hot butter mixture. Fry each pancake for 2 to 3 minutes on each side or until they are crisp and golden. The pancakes are served hot with cranberry sauce.

ARROWHEAD SOUP WITH CUCUMBERS

10 egg-sized arrowhead tubers	1 cup heavy cream
Juice of 2 lemons	1 cup milk
2 small cucumbers	2 tablespoons wild onion, finely
3 cups cold water	chopped
1½ teaspoons salt	2 tablespoons fresh dill, finely
¼ teaspoon black pepper	chopped

Scrub the arrowhead tubers well under running water. Peel the tubers, making sure the skin only is removed. Cut them in ½-inch slices. Drop tubers into a bowl of water into which the lemon juice has been squeezed.

Peel the cucumbers and slice lengthwise into halves. Take out the seeds by running the tip of a spoon down the centre of the cucumber. Cut the cucumber into ¼-inch slices and set aside.

Using a heavy 3 or 4-quart saucepan, bring water to a boil and drop in the tubers. Reduce the heat, add salt and pepper and cook covered for 30 minutes or until the arrowhead tubers feel soft and can be mashed against the sides of the pan. Pour contents of the pot into a sieve placed over a mixing bowl, and with a wooden spoon force the tubers through the sieve.

Return the purée and the cooking liquid to the saucepan and stir in the cream, milk and onion. Simmer over low heat for 5 minutes or until the soup is smooth, then add the cucumber and simmer for 10 minutes more or until the cucumber is tender but still very firm. Do not overcook the cucumber, as it will take away that piquant smell and taste.

In the last 2 or 3 minutes add the dill.

Serve hot from individual soup bowls.

ARROWHEAD HASH

10 egg-sized arrowhead tubers	Salt and pepper
1 pound cooked roast beef	2 tablespoons finely chopped
½ pound smoked ham	canned beets
5 tablespoons butter	6 eggs
2 wild onions, finely chopped	

Brush and clean the arrowhead tubers, peel as thinly as possible, and put into a 2-quart saucepan with water to cover and a little salt. Bring to a boil, turn the heat down and simmer for 15 minutes. Drain the tubers and cool to room temperature.

When they are cold, dice in ¼-inch cubes. Do the same with the roast beef and smoked ham.

Melt 2 tablespoons of butter in a 12-inch skillet until it gives off a nutty aroma, add the onions and fry until they are brown but not burned. Remove the onions and put to one side. Drop in another tablespoon of butter and fry the tubers until they are crisp and golden.

Remove from skillet with a slotted spoon and drain on a double thickness of paper towels. Drop in another tablespoon of butter, add the diced meat and fry for about 10 minutes. Add another tablespoon of butter, return the onions and fry over low heat for another 5 minutes. Shake the pan often to brown the meat on all sides and to get it thoroughly heated. Finally, add the tubers and let the whole dish simmer for 15 minutes, adding salt and pepper to taste. Just before serving, add the chopped beets to give a little color.

Arrange individual servings of the hash on warm plates, making a hole in each serving to take a fried egg. The eggs should be fried sunny-side up and transferred without breaking from the skillet to the serving plates.

Or you may do as I do — serve the dish with raw eggs. Place a raw egg yolk in a half egg shell and nestle the shell in the centre of the hash. People will then mix the raw egg with the hash themselves.

JERUSALEM ARTICHOKE

(Helianthus tuberosus)

This plant grows with thin stalks commonly 3 to 5 feet tall. The rough leaves, whose tops are hairy, develop sharp points from an egg-shaped body that is broadest near the base. The frequently numerous flowers are yellow, 2 to 3 inches wide, and mature on slender stems that rise from where the higher leaves meet the stalk. The blossom lacks the brownish centre of those sunflowers which yield edible seeds.

JERUSALEM ARTICHOKE

115

Wild Jerusalem artichoke should be harvested before late. fall. It is a native of the central part of United States and Canada. The plant was a popular vegetable among the Indians, and when the Europeans arrived in this country they cultivated it, which explains why it is so widespread. History is all in favor of this delicacy, but it may take you a while to get accustomed to its sweet juiciness. The tubers are considered so nutritious and digestible that they are regarded as an excellent food for invalids.

IN THE BUSH

As a Cooked Vegetable: The tubers are good simmered in their skins in as little water as will cover them. Peel and serve them as you would potatoes, with butter or margarine.

Jerusalem artichoke chips are also delicious. Parboil a pound of the unpeeled artichokes. Before they are quite tender, take them off the fire and rub off the skins. Dry the artichokes well and slice thinly. Fry in porcupine fat until golden brown.

As a Salad: The Jerusalem artichoke makes an excellent salad — one you will never forget. Boil the tubers first, then mix 4 or 5 tubers with 2 or 3 finely sliced wild onions, 2 stalks of bulrush shoots chopped finely, some salt and a cup of birch tree sap.

HOME RECIPES

STUFFED JERUSALEM ARTICHOKES

6 medium-sized roots	Salt and pepper
½ lemon	2 teaspoons nutmeg
1 small wild onion, finely chopped	2 tablespoons parsley
2 tablespoons butter	½ cup grated cheese
1 4-ounce can sliced mushrooms	1 can consommé

Clean and scrape the tubers well. Put in a 3-quart saucepan and cover with water. Press the lemon and add the juice to prevent the tubers from blackening. Add a little salt and bring to a boil. Simmer for 15 minutes, then drain. Cooking the tubers in too high heat or for too long will toughen them.

Lightly fry the chopped onion in the butter. Add the mushrooms and stir over a brisk fire until the butter has completely evaporated. Season with salt, pepper and nutmeg and add the finely chopped parsley, mixing thoroughly.

Transfer to a bowl, cover with a piece of wax paper and put to one side.

Preheat oven to 425°. Take the tubers and peel them. Make a hole in each and fill with the stuffing. Arrange them in a buttered casserole, sprinkle with a little grated cheese, add the can of consommé and put into the oven for 25 minutes. Serve with a Madeira sauce or add some Madeira to the casserole 5 minutes before taking the dish out of the oven.

JERUSALEM ARTICHOKE SOUP

8 Jerusalem artichoke tubers	2 egg yolks
2 tablespoons lemon juice	1 tablespoon sugar
5 cups milk	1 teaspoon salt

Peel the tubers and put in a 3-quart stainless steel saucepan filled with water to which the lemon juice has been added. Bring to a boil and simmer for 15 minutes. Drain the tubers and save the cooking juices.

Using the same saucepan, bring the milk to a simmer but make sure it doesn't come to a boil. Break the egg yolks into a cup and add to the milk, stirring constantly with a wire whisk. Add 2½ cups of the saved fluid to the milk and egg mixture. Slice the tubers in ½-inch slices and add to the mixture. Add the sugar and salt. Let stand on the hot stove, making sure it does not come to a boil, for 10 minutes. Serve with finely chopped parsley in individual bowls.

JERUSALEM ARTICHOKES SUZETTE

10 Jerusalem artichoke tubers	2 egg yolks
Juice of a lemon	4 tablespoons thick cream
Salt and pepper	1 chicken breast, boiled
2 tablespoons butter	1 4-ounce can mushrooms

Preheat oven to 425°. Peel some fine medium-sized tubers, turning each into the shape of an egg. As you peel them put them into a saucepan filled with water and the lemon juice. Cut them flat at one end so that they will stand upright. Place them in a thick-bottomed frying pan and put them in the oven for 45 minutes.

After they are baked, open them like a boiled egg and take out the pulp. Save the tops. When taking out the pulp, make sure the walls and the bottom of the tubers are not thinner than ¼ inch all around.

Season the pulp and mash it in a bowl, adding the butter and egg yolks. Gradually work in the cream. Chop the parboiled chicken breast into small pieces and add to the mixture together with the well-drained and chopped mushrooms. Fill the Jerusalem artichoke tubers with the mixture. Put the saved covers back on and place them back in the frying pan in the oven for another 15 minutes at 400°. When ready to serve, set on a dish and glaze with butter.

JERUSALEM ARTICHOKES WITH PHEASANT

2 pheasants	1 teaspoon ginger
2 large cooking apples, diced	½ cup butter
4 wild onions, minced	½ teaspoon pepper
1 teaspoon salt	1 cup orange juice
3 cups soft bread crumbs	1 cup drained plum juice
1 15-ounce can purple plums	1 cup dry white wine
1 cup chopped dried apricots	Jerusalem artichoke chips

Pluck and draw the pheasants and wash thoroughly inside and out. In a mixing bowl combine the apples, onions, ½ teaspoon salt, bread crumbs, the drained and stoned plums, apricots and ginger. When the ingredients are well mixed, place the mixture in the cavities of the pheasants and store in the refrigerator overnight.

Next day preheat the oven to 400°. Sew up the cavities and truss the birds with kitchen string. Melt the butter and blend it with the salt and pepper in a small bowl. Rub this mixture well into the outer skin of the pheasants. Place the birds breast up in an uncovered roasting pan and add the leftover salt-butter mixture, the orange juice and juice from the plums.

Put in the oven for 20 minutes to give the pheasants a golden-brown color, then reduce the heat to 325° and cover the roasting pan. Using a bulb baster, baste the pheasants every 10 minutes with the juices from the pan. Cook an additional 1½ hours. While they are cooking prepare the Jerusalem artichoke chips.

JERUSALEM ARTICHOKE CHIPS

4 cups vegetable oil	Juice of 2 lemons
10 medium-sized Jerusalem artichokes	2 teaspoons salt

Line a jelly roll pan or large shallow roasting pan with a double thickness of paper towels. In a large, heavy saucepan heat the oil until a haze forms above it.

Wash and clean the Jerusalem artichoke tubers, peel them as thinly as possible and drop them into a saucepan with water to which the lemon juice has been added to prevent the tubers from discoloring. With a sharp knife cut the tubers crosswise in sixteenth-inch slices and drop them into the water again.

When all the tubers have been sliced and the oil is hot, drain the tubers in a large colander and pat the slices dry on a paper towel.

Drop about ¼ cup of tubers at a time into the hot oil and turn them with a slotted spoon. Fry for 3 to 4 mintues or until they are crisp and golden brown. Transfer the chips to the paper-lined pan and keep them warm until serving time. Sprinkle with salt.

When the birds are cooked, place on a heated platter, remove strings with a sharp knife, and arrange the chips in a circle around them.

Scrape the bottom of the roasting pan well and add the dry white wine. Over low heat add 2 tablespoons of flour to the cooking fluid and stir until the sauce is smooth and creamy. Cook for 10 minutes. Strain the sauce and serve in a gravy boat.

BAKED JERUSALEM ARTICHOKE OMELET

4 medium-sized Jerusalem artichoke tubers	4 eggs
	½ teaspoon salt
Juice of a lemon	3 tablespoons butter

Clean and scrape the artichokes. In a 2-quart saucepan cover the artichokes with 1 quart water and the lemon juice and bring to a boil. Lower the heat and cook for 15 minutes, then remove the tubers and peel them. Preheat the oven to 425°. Heat the butter in a 10-inch skillet over high heat. When it gives off a nutty aroma, lower the heat, quarter the Jerusalem artichokes lengthwise and add them to the pan.

Cook over moderate heat for 10 minutes or until they are golden brown. In a small bowl mix the eggs and salt with a beater until they are frothy. Butter a 1-quart casserole and place the artichokes on the bottom. Pour the beaten eggs over them. Bake in the upper half of the oven for 20 minutes or until the omelet is firm and golden brown.

Serve at once.

JERUSALEM ARTICHOKES WITH DUCK

4 to 5-pound duck	**10 Jerusalem artichoke tubers**
1 teaspoon salt	**Juice of a lemon**
¼ teaspoon pepper	**1 cup dry white wine**
2 tart cooking apples	**1 cup chicken stock**
4 tablespoons butter	**2 tablespoons flour**
1 wild onion, thinly sliced	

Preheat the oven to 350°. Wash the duck under running water and dry with paper towels. Rub the cavity with salt and pepper. Chop the cooking apples coarsely and fill the cavity. Truss the duck neatly.

In a heavy 12-inch skillet melt 2 tablespoons butter over high heat. When it gives off a nutty aroma, lower the heat and cook the onion for 10 minutes. Remove with a slotted spoon and set aside. Brown the duck on all sides in the pan, using 2 spoons to turn it.

In a heavy fireproof casserole large enough to take the duck and with a cover, melt 2 tablespoons of butter over low heat. When the butter has melted, cover the bottom of the casserole with the browned onion and place the duck on top. Cover and put in the oven for 1 hour. In the meantime, scrape and peel the artichokes and drop them into a bowl of water and the lemon juice.

Remove the duck from the casserole and strain the juices through a fine sieve, pressing down hard on the onions. Let the juice settle and skim off as much of the surface fat as possible. Return the duck to the casserole and place the peeled artichokes around it. Add the juices, the wine and the chicken stock. The liquid should cover the artichokes. Bring to a simmer on top of the stove, cover the casserole and put in the middle of the oven. Cook for 35 to 40 minutes, or until the artichoke is tender when pierced with the tip of a sharp knife. Remove the duck to a rack set in a shallow roasting pan and return to the oven for 10 minutes to glaze to a deep brown. Cut off the trussing strings and place the duck on a heated platter. Arrange the artichokes around the duck or at one end of the platter. Skim as much surface fat off as possible from the braising sauce and taste for seasoning. Scrape the sides and bottom of the casserole, add the flour, and stir until smooth and creamy. Simmer for 10 minutes and strain through a fine sieve. Serve the sauce in a gravy boat. Sprinkle with parsley. As a complement serve cranberry sauce.

JERUSALEM ARTICHOKES WITH ANCHOVY FILLETS

10 medium Jerusalem artichoke tubers	**2 tablespoons butter, cut in ¼-inch pieces**
Juice of 2 lemons	**2 tablespoons fine dry bread crumbs**
4 tablespoons butter	
6 wild onions, thinly sliced	**½ cup milk**
20 flat anchovy fillets	**1 cup heavy cream**
White pepper	

Preheat the oven to 375°. Scrape and peel the artichokes and drop them into a bowl of water to which the lemon juice has been added. This is to keep the tubers from discoloring. Heat 2 tablespoons of butter in a 12-inch heavy skillet over high heat. When it gives off a nutty aroma, lower the heat and add the onions. Cook for 10 minutes, until they are golden brown. Cut the artichokes tubers in 2-inch lengths and ¼-inch slices. Pat them dry with paper towels.

With a pastry brush spread the remaining butter in the bottom and sides of a 2-quart baking dish. Place a layer of artichoke slices on the bottom of the dish and then alternate layers of onions and anchovies, ending with a layer of artichokes slices. Sprinkle each layer with a little white pepper and small pieces of butter. Scatter the bread crumbs on top of the artichokes and dot with small pieces of butter. Add the milk and the heavy cream to the dish and put it into the oven. Bake in the center of the oven for 1 hour or until the artichokes are tender. If the crust seems to be getting too dark, cover the dish with a piece of aluminum foil.

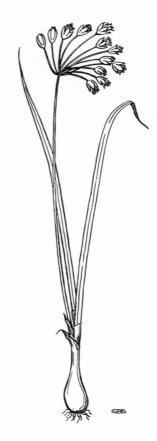

WILD ONION

WILD ONION

(Allium spp.*)*

The leaves of this plant are broad and elliptical, and appear in early spring. They disappear before the flowers emerge. The flowers grow in umbel-like clusters and vary in color from a light pink to purple. The stem and leaves are of a fresh green color when young. Upon maturation, however, they tend to become gray or yellow.

The root and stem of the wild onion are excellent both raw and cooked. The plant can be prepared by any method used to prepare domestic onion.

The onion is a very nutritious food and should be added to the diet whenever possible. It also has the advantage over many other vegetables that it can be dried and stored for future use.

A thick syrup can be made by boiling down the juice of the onion which is beneficial as a soothing syrup for an irritated throat.

IN THE BUSH

CRISP ONION RINGS

Peel the wild onions and slice about ¼ inch thick. If you are close to a creek with ice-cold water, put the onion rings in a bag and submerge them.

Pound some bulrush seeds to flour between two stones. Remove the onion rings from the water and drain them well. Melt some porcupine fat and bring to a boil. Dip the onion rings in the bulrush flour and fry until nicely browned. To keep the rings hot, put them on a piece of aluminum foil close to the fire.

ONION CASSEROLE

Make a box out of a piece of aluminum foil. Put 8 to 10 medium-sized onions, peeled and sliced, into the bottom of your makeshift casserole. Cover the onion with wild mustard seed and put a layer of peeled and sliced Jerusalem artichokes on top. If you have some stock from a previously cooked bird, pour this over the casserole and cover with a large leaf of some kind.

Rake some of the coals of your fire to the side and on the remaining coals place a flat stone large enough to take the casserole. Place stones all around the casserole and finish with another flat stone on top. Seal all the cracks between the stones with clay or mud, and rake the coals back over the oven. Let stand for a couple of hours.

HOME RECIPES

WILD ONION AND POTATO SOUP WITH PEPPERONI

½ pound wild spring onions	½ cup olive oil
3 medium-sized potatoes	¼ teaspoon freshly ground pepper
6 cups water	1 4-ounce package of pepperoni
2 teaspoons salt	

Peel and clean the wild onions; peel the potatoes and slice in ¼-inch rounds. Put them in a 4 to 5-quart saucepan with the water and salt, and bring to a boil over high heat. Reduce the heat to moderate and cook uncovered for 30 minutes or until the onions can easily be mashed against the sides of the pan. With a slotted spoon, transfer the onions and potatoes to a bowl and mash them to a smooth purée with a fork.

Return the onions and potatoes to the liquid in the pan, stir in the olive oil and pepper and bring to a boil. Reduce the heat and let simmer.

Place the pepperoni in a small skillet and prick it in two or three places with the point of a knife. Add enough water to cover it and bring to boil over high heat. Reduce the heat and simmer for 15 minutes. Drain the pepperoni on paper towels; slice into ¼-inch rounds.

After the pepperoni is well drained, add it to the onion mixture and serve hot with croutons.

STUFFED WILD ONIONS

10 large wild onions	½ cup finely chopped onions
½ cup fresh bread crumbs	1 pound lean ground beef
¼ cup heavy cream	5 tablespoons butter
1 egg	2 tablespoons molasses
1 teaspoon salt	2 tablespoons bread crumbs
¼ teaspoon pepper	

Put the peeled wild onions in a 3 to 4-quart saucepan and cover with water. Bring to a boil over moderate heat. Lower the heat and simmer for 30 minutes.

In the meantime, make the stuffing. Put the ½ cup of bread crumbs in a large bowl and add the heavy cream. Soak for 5 minutes. Add the egg and the salt and pepper. Mix the ingredients well. Add the chopped onions and the ground beef. Knead with both hands or beat with a wooden spoon until all the ingredients are well mixed. Set aside. Remove the onions from the pot with a slotted spoon. Drain them and let them cool on a platter. With a sharp knife, slit a cross in the top of each onion about ½ an inch deep. By pulling on the skin in the direction opposite to your slit, the onion should separate easily. Try not to increase the slit. Discard the inner part of the onion, as it is usually too small to take any filling. Put the stuffing in the onion cases. Roll onions in 2 tablespoons melted butter.

Preheat the oven to 375°. In a 1½ to 2-quart flameproof casserole, melt 3 tablespoons of butter on top of the stove. Using a pastry brush, make sure the sides and the bottom are well greased. Remove the casserole from the heat and place the onion rolls in it side by side. Pour the molasses on top of the onion rolls and put the dish in the oven. Bake for 20 minutes and then baste the onion rolls with the butter and molasses from the bottom of the casserole. Baste again in 20 minutes and sprinkle the 2 tablespoons of bread crumbs over the rolls.

Place the casserole back in the oven for another 20 minutes, or until the rolls are slightly browned.

ROULADES OF VENISON WITH ANCHOVIES AND ONION

2 pounds round steak of venison	1 teaspoon salt
4 tablespoons butter	½ teaspoon pepper
4 tablespoons vegetable oil	20 flat anchovy fillets
2 cups minced wild onion	½ cup water
2 tablespoons flour	1 cup dry red wine

Cut the meat in slices about 6 by 3 inches and using a meat pounder, pound the steaks into ¼-inch thickness. Trim to the above size.

In an 8-inch heavy skillet, heat 1 tablespoon of butter and 2 tablespoons vegetable oil. Add the chopped onions and sauté for 10 minutes or until they are golden brown. Remove from heat and stir in the flour. Return to the heat and cook for 4 to 5 minutes. Reserve 3 tablespoons of this roux for the sauce. Sprinkle each slice of meat with salt and pepper and spread the roux evenly over the meat. Place 3 anchovy fillets on each slice and roll the slices up securely. Tie with a piece of kitchen string around each end.

Heat the remaining butter and oil in a 2-quart flameproof casserole over moderate heat on top of the stove. Add all the roulades and cook for 8 minutes, turning them with kitchen tongs. Make sure they are well browned on all sides.

Preheat the oven to 325°. Pour the water and wine into the casserole and add the roux you have reserved. Cover tightly and bake for 1 hour. Serve this dish from the casserole with mashed arrowhead tubers and a dish of sour cream to which finely chopped leeks have been added.

ONIONS AND BEEF BRAISED IN BEER

8 strips of bacon, diced	2 bay leaves
5 tablespoons butter	4 tablespoons flour
8 cups thinly sliced wild onion	3 cups beer or ale
3 pounds boneless moose chuck, cut in 2-inch chunks	1½ cups beef stock
2 tablespoons butter	½ cup dry red wine
1 teaspoon salt	1½ teaspoons sugar
½ teaspoon pepper	2 tablespoons chopped parsley

Put the diced bacon in a heavy 12-inch skillet and bring to high heat. Lower the heat and cook until the fat is rendered and the bacon is golden brown. Remove with a slotted spoon and set aside. Drain almost all the fat from the skillet into a small bowl and set aside. In another 12-inch skillet, melt 5 tablespoons of butter over high heat. When it gives off a nutty aroma, lower the heat and add the sliced onions. Cover and let simmer for 30 minutes, stirring occasionally to make sure the onions are not sticking to the bottom of the skillet.

While the onions are cooking heat the bacon fat in the first skillet just until it starts to smoke. Add the moose chunks a few at a time, making sure the meat is not crowded. Brown the meat on all sides to a rich brown. Remove with a slotted spoon and set aside. As moose meat is very lean, you have to add more bacon fat as you proceed. In a Dutch oven melt 2 tablespoons of butter. Place the browned moose meat into the melted butter. Add the salt and pepper and the 2 bay leaves. When all the moose meat is browned, stir the flour into the remaining fat and make a smooth paste. If it seems too thick, add some more fat and a little water. Return the skillet to very low heat and cook for 10 more minutes. Be careful not to burn the roux. Remove from heat, pour the beer into the skillet, constantly stirring. Add the beef stock and the wine. Make sure all ingredients are well mixed. Over low heat, mix the sugar into the roux; stir vigorously for 2 minutes.

Preheat oven to 350°. Season to taste with salt and pepper. When the onions are ready, add them to the moose meat in the Dutch oven and pour the sauce over top. Stir the mixture very gently just to get all the ingredients well mixed. The sauce should cover the meat. If it doesn't, add some more beer. Bring the mixture to a boil on top of the stove. Cover the Dutch oven carefully. If the lid does not fit tightly, press a piece of aluminium foil down over the sides and then place the lid on top. Place the Dutch oven in the lower part of the oven and regulate the heat so the mixture simmers gently for 2 hours or until the meat is tender when pierced with the tip of a sharp knife. Before serving, let the dish cool for 5 minutes.

Skim the surface fat and discard the bay leaves. Sprinkle the dish with the finely chopped parsley.

PICKLED WILD ONIONS

1 cup white vinegar	1 teaspoon celery seeds
1 cup sugar	1 teaspoon mustard seeds
¼ teaspoon ground cloves	¼ teaspoon salt
1 cinnamon stick	10 wild onions

In a heavy stainless steel 2-quart saucepan, mix the vinegar, sugar, cloves, cinnamon stick, celery seed, mustard seed and salt. Bring to a boil. Lower the temperature and simmer for 15 minutes. Cool. Peel and slice the onions in ¼-inch slices and put into a clean jar with a screw lid.

Add the syrup when it is cool. Chill at least 24 hours before using.

FRENCH FRIED WILD ONION RINGS

10 wild onions	2 tablespoons vegetable oil
½ cup flour	1 egg
½ teaspoon salt	½ tablespoon milk
½ teaspoon baking powder	4 cups vegetable oil for frying

Peel the onions, slice ¼-inch thick, and separate into rings. Put aside. Combine the flour, salt and baking powder in a medium-sized mixing bowl. Add the vegetable oil and stir until smooth. In another bowl, beat the egg until fluffy and add the milk slowly. When well mixed, combine with the flour mixture. Using an electric beater, beat until smooth and thick.

Heat the oil in a deep fryer or kettle to about 365°. Make sure the oil is at least 3 inches from the top of the fryer to prevent it from boiling over when the onion rings are added.

Dip the onion rings in the batter and fry 4 or 5 at a time until golden brown. Drain on a double layer of paper towels. Keep hot until used. Be sure to keep the oil hot between batches.

GLAZED ONIONS IN WHITE SAUCE

2 pounds small wild onions	¼ cup heavy cream
1 can beef consommé	1¼ teaspoons salt
4 tablespoons butter	¼ teaspoon pepper
1 cup flour	2 tablespoons sugar
½ cup white table wine	2 tablespoons butter
2 cups milk	2 hard-boiled eggs

Peel the onions without cutting them. Put the consommé in a 2-quart saucepan and bring to a boil. Add the onions and enough water to cover them. Boil for 30 minutes. Drain and set aside.

In a 2-quart saucepan, melt the butter over moderate heat. Remove from the heat and stir in the flour, making sure you get a smooth heavy paste. Add wine and mix thoroughly. Pour in milk and cream all at once, stirring constantly with a wire whisk.

Place over low heat and cook until the sauce is smooth and thick. Season with the salt and pepper.

In a frying pan melt the sugar and butter, making sure the sugar doesn't burn. Add the onions. Roll them around to cover them on all sides. When they are fully covered, add them to the white sauce and simmer for 10 minutes until they are thoroughly heated. Garnish with rounds of hard-boiled egg.

ONION AND RICE SOUP

1 teaspoon salt	1 can cream of mushroom soup
½ pound wild rice	1 cup milk
1 pound wild onions	1 teaspoon sugar
6 slices bacon	1 cup heavy cream

Put 1 quart of water in a 2-quart saucepan, bring to a boil and add the salt. Stir the rice into the boiling water slowly so the water never stops bubbling. Cover and simmer for 35 minutes or until a kernel of rice pressed between your fingers is soft. Drain and let stand with lid on.

Chop the onion finely and cook in butter for 15 minutes. Line the bottom and sides of a medium saucepan with the bacon. Spoon the rice and onions into the pan and add the soup, milk and sugar. Cover and cook gently for ½ hour.

There are two ways to serve this soup.

1. Drain through a sieve and save the liquid. Put contents of sieve in blender for 2 or 3 minutes, then rub this purée through a fine sieve again. Put the purée back into the liquid and add the heavy cream. If necessary, add a little milk to get the right consistency, but this soup should be thick.

2. Drain through a sieve and save the liquid. Remove bacon strips and chop finely. Put bacon, onion and rice back into the liquid and add the heavy cream. Stir and simmer for 10 minutes.

This soup should be thinner than the first one but not too thin.

Garnish with finely chopped chives.

YELLOW WATERLILY

YELLOW WATERLILY

(Nuphar variegatum)

Yellow waterlily leaves are oval or round with a deep curve at the heart-shaped base. They may be either floating or erect. The flowers are flattened globes made up of half a dozen thick golden sepals arching over the stamen-like petals.

The yellow waterlily has many names: cow lily, spatterdock or the Indian name wokas. The Klamath Indians often used the seeds as a staple food, and they are still a favorite delicacy today. The squaws usually go out in canoes to the lily patches and pick the full-grown pods while they are hard, or scoop up the already opened ones with a wicker spoon. The pods are then deposited in holes in the ground, where they ferment and turn into a mucilaginous mass from which the seeds may be freed by washing. The seeds are then prepared in various ways for eating, either cooked as a mush or meal or merely parched. They are delicious prepared in this manner.

The roots are also edible and were often boiled or roasted by the Indians. They used to gather them in great quantities from the muskrat houses, where they had been stored for the winter. Many people consider the flavor of the yellow waterlily roots too strong, but this can be changed by boiling in two changes of water or by seasoning.

IN THE BUSH

As a Cooked Vegetable: My favorite way to prepare the waterlily roots is to wash them well and then scrape them with a knife to remove all the black spots. I wrap them with meat in aluminium foil and put them in the hot coals of the campfire for about 2 hours. Or they can be put in the hot embers in the morning, and supper is ready when you return from hunting in the afternoon.

As Popcorn: The yellow waterlily seeds can be popped, and with some fat or butter added, they are tastier than popcorn in my estimation. Simply take the pods and remove the green holster and you will have a handful of seeds. Wrap them in aluminium foil and put them close to the fire. Soon you will hear the familiar popping sound and in a few minutes they are ready to eat.

HOME RECIPES

YELLOW POND LILY STEW

3 pounds stewing beef	Salt and pepper
3 or 4 wild onions	2 cups water
10 to 12 yellow pond lily roots	¼ cup dry red wine
3 tablespoons clarified butter	2 tablespoons flour

Cut the meat in fairly even slices about ½ inch thick. Peel and mince the onions, slice the lily roots.

Brown the onions in a pan using clarified butter. Pound the meat thoroughly and brown in pan fat. Place alternate layers of lily root slices, meat and onions in a 3 or 4-quart saucepan, making the bottom and top layers of lily roots. Season rather well. Add water to remains in the frying pan, stir well and pour over the meat mixture, leaving a little in the pan with which to make a sauce.

Cover tightly and simmer for 2 to 3 hours. Just before the dish is finished add the dry red wine. Drain off the cooking fluid and put into the frying pan, blend in flour to thicken the sauce and add salt and pepper to taste. Simmer for five minutes, then pour the sauce over the dish. Serve hot.

CRUSTY MOLDED YELLOW POND LILY ROOTS

8 tablespoons butter	1 teaspoon pepper
2½ pounds lily roots	1 teaspoon finely chopped parsley
1 teaspoon salt	Egg sauce

First clarify the butter in a small saucepan by melting slowly over low heat. Spoon the clarified butter off the top and put it into a bowl. Discard the white milky solids at the bottom of the pan.

In a 3 or 4-quart saucepan place the lily roots, cover with water and add a little salt. Bring to a boil over high heat, lower the heat and cook for 15 minutes. Drain the water. Refill with fresh water and a little salt, bring to a boil and cook for a further 20 minutes. Drain the water and let the lily roots cool to room temperature.

When they are cool, peel and slice the roots in ¼-inch slices. In a heavy 8 or 10-inch skillet with sloping sides and a cover, heat 2 tablespoons of clarified butter over low heat, swirling it around to coat the bottom and sides very well. Remove the skillet from the heat and place a layer of lily root slices in concentric circles, each slice overlapping the last. With a pastry brush spread a little butter on top of the slices. Season them lightly with salt and pepper. Then shake the skillet gently back and forth to make sure the slices are not stuck to the bottom of the pan. Cook them over low heat for half a minute to melt the butter and set the slices.

Take off the heat and arrange a second layer in concentric circles on top of the first, brush with butter and add salt and pepper. Continue to build up layers until the pan is full. Shake the pan gently to make sure the bottom layers are not sticking. Pour the remaining butter over the dish, cover and cook for 30 minutes or until the roots are tender when pierced with the tip of a sharp knife.

When the lily roots are done, remove the cover and slide a narrow spatula along the sides of the skillet, freeing any of the slices which may have stuck to the sides.

Gently force the spatula along the bottom of the skillet without disrupting the pattern. Place a round heated platter upside down on the skillet, hold the platter and skillet together, and reverse them quickly.

The lily roots should emerge as a round, compact cake. If any slices have stuck to the bottom, remove them from the skillet and place on the ring of the cake where they belong.

Serve this dish with egg sauce and mustard.

EGG SAUCE

3 tablespoons butter	Salt and pepper
4 tablespoons flour	1 tablespoon dry mustard
1 cup milk	2 teaspoons sugar
2 hard-boiled eggs, finely chopped	1 tablespoon whiskey

In a 2-quart saucepan, melt the butter over high heat. When the foam subsides add the flour and stir briskly with a whisk. Add the milk a little at a time until you have a smooth heavy cream. Simmer for 10 minutes, stirring constantly and making sure the sauce does not stick to the bottom of the pan. Add the finely chopped eggs, season to taste, and finally add the dry mustard mixed with the sugar and whiskey.

Pour over the lily cake as hot as possible.

YELLOW WATERLILY POPCORN

½ pound waterlily seeds	2 tablespoons butter
1 teaspoon salt	

Use a 4 to 5-quart soup kettle filled with water to separate the seeds from the floaters. Simply take the pods, break away the green holsters and dump all the seeds into the water. The seeds will float, but after 5 to 6 hours the floaters will give up their grip on the seeds, which will then sink to the bottom of the kettle. Skim off the surface and you will have all the seeds on the bottom of the kettle. Drain the water off in a sieve and spread the seeds on a cookie sheet. Place in a 150° oven to dry — if you use more heat, the seeds will start to pop on you.

Using an ordinary popper, quarter fill it with dried seeds. Pop on the stove as you would ordinary corn. Melt the butter in a 2-quart saucepan, add the salt, stir and pour over the popped waterlily seeds. Stir the seeds around so all of them are covered by the butter.

SCALLOPED POND LILY ROOTS WITH CHEESE

10 to 12 pond lily roots	1 teaspoon salt
1 clove garlic	¼ teaspoon pepper
1½ cups grated cheese	1¼ cups milk
6 tablespoons butter	

Place the peeled lily roots in a 3 or 4-quart saucepan, add water and a little salt, bring to a boil, lower the heat and cook for 15 minutes. Drain the water and let the roots cool to room temperature.

Preheat the oven to 450°. Rub the bottom and sides of a 10 by 12-inch fireproof casserole with 2-inch sides with the bruised garlic and grease lightly with butter. Slice the lily roots in ¼-inch slices and cover the bottom of the casserole with them. Sprinkle with half the cheese, butter, salt and pepper. Spread the rest of the lily slices on top of the cheese and sprinkle the rest of the cheese over the top of the dish. Place bits of butter on top and season with the rest of the salt and pepper. Pour the milk on top of the casserole. Bring to a simmer over low heat and then bake in the middle of the oven for 25 minutes or until the lily roots feel tender when pierced with the tip of a sharp knife.

Remove all the excess fluid with a bulb baster and bake for another 5 minutes or until the top is nicely browned. Serve at once.

GLAZED POND LILY ROOTS

10 to 12 medium lily roots	½ teaspoon salt
1½ cups beef stock	½ teaspoon pepper
4 tablespoons butter	2 tablespoons finely chopped
4 tablespoons honey	parsley

Place the scraped and peeled lily roots in a 3-quart saucepan and cover with water. Add a little salt, bring to a boil and simmer for 15 minutes.

Drain the water and replace. Bring to a boil again, moderate the heat and simmer for 10 minutes.

In a heavy 8 to 10-inch skillet, combine the beef stock, butter, honey, salt and pepper, and bring to a boil over a moderate heat.

Take the lily roots from the water and with a sharp knife form the roots into cylinders about 1 inch in diameter. Return to the skillet, cover, and simmer over low heat, shaking the skillet occasionally to roll the lily roots about in the liquid. Check to see that the liquid is not cooking away too fast. In 30 minutes the lily roots should be tender when pierced with the tip of a sharp knife. The braising liquid should be brown and shiny. If the stock has not reduced enough, remove the lily roots with a slotted spoon and put to one side. Then boil down the mixture over high heat. Before serving, transfer the lily roots back into the skillet and roll them around to coat them again.

Remove the lily roots to a platter and pour the cooking juices over them. Sprinkle with the finely chopped parsley.

YELLOW WATERLILY CAKE

3 waterlily roots	2 teaspoons cinnamon
8 tablespoons butter	3 eggs
2 cups old cheese, grated	1 tablespoon bread crumbs
4 tablespoons honey	½ - 1 cup grated cheese

Peel the waterlily roots, cut in half crosswise and in ¼-inch slices lengthwise. Using a 12-inch heavy skillet, melt 4 tablespoons butter over high heat. When it gives off a nutty aroma, lower the heat and add the sliced roots. Cook for 15 minutes or until the roots are golden brown on all sides. Transfer to a double thickness of paper towel and drain. In a mixing bowl mix the grated cheese, honey and cinnamon. Use an electric beater and beat rather well. Break the eggs over the bowl one at a time and mix thoroughly after adding each. Preheat the oven to 325°. Grease the bottom and sides of a deep 1-quart baking mold, add the bread crumbs and shake well so the sides are well covered. Knock the mold on the edge of the table to remove any excess bread crumbs.

Ladle about a quarter of the egg mixture into the mold and spread it evenly on the bottom with a wooden spoon. Cover with a layer of waterlily roots. Sprinkle with a ¼ cup of cheese and dot with 1 tablespoon butter.

Repeat the layers until all the egg mixture and waterlily roots are used, ending with a layer of the egg mixture. Dot the top of the mold with the remaining butter. Place the mold in the middle of the oven and bake for 40 minutes. Unmold and serve hot.

BAKED YELLOW WATERLILY IN CREAM WITH CHEESE

1 cup dry white wine	¼ teaspoon nutmeg
2 tablespoons wild onion, minced	¼ teaspoon cayenne pepper
2 pounds waterlily roots	1½ teaspoons salt
2 tablespoons bread crumbs	¼ teaspoon pepper
6 tablespoons light cream	¾ cup old, sharp cheese, grated
6 tablespoons butter	2 hard-cooked eggs, quartered
6 tablespoons flour	lengthwise
¼ teaspoon paprika	

In a 3 or 4-quart saucepan combine the wine and onion, bring to a boil over high heat, reduce the heat to a simmer and cook for 7 minutes.

Scrape and peel the waterlily roots, cut in quarters lengthwise, and chop into 1-inch pieces. Add to the saucepan and cook for 15 minutes or until the roots feel soft. Drain the waterlily roots through a sieve over a mixing bowl and set to one side both the roots and the cooking fluid.

Preheat the oven to 325°. In a small bowl soak the bread crumbs in 2 tablespoons of cream. Melt the butter in a heavy 2 to 3-quart saucepan over high heat. When it gives off a nutty aroma, reduce the heat and stir in the flour, stirring constantly for 3 minutes. Stir in the saved cooking fluid and the remaining cream very slowly. Cook over high heat, stirring all the time until the sauce thickens and comes to a boil. Add the soaked bread crumbs, paprika, nutmeg, cayenne, salt and pepper and stir until all the ingredients are well mixed. Stir in ½ cup of the grated cheese and cook for 5 minutes, add the waterlily roots and cook for another 5 minutes.

Butter the sides and bottom of a 2-quart baking dish and arrange the hard-cooked eggs in the bottom. Spoon in the waterlily mixture and smooth the surface with a wooden spoon. Sprinkle the remaining cheese on top of the dish and bake in the middle of the oven for 30 minutes or until the mixture boils and bubbles and is brown on top.

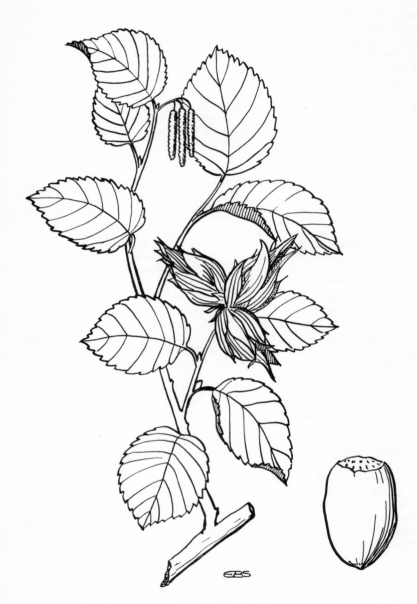

BEAKED HAZLENUT

BEAKED HAZELNUT

(Corylus cornuta)

The beaked hazelnut is a shrub or small tree which grows in clumps, its widely spreading branches reaching a height of up to 7 feet. The alternate short-stemmed leaves, which resemble those of the yellow birch and alder, are egg-shaped or oval, with sharp tips and toothed margins.

Three species of hazelnut are natives of the United States and Canada. Two grow in the east and one is found in the Rockies. Incidently, the filberts sold in the stores are cultivated hazelnuts. The best nuts come from Spain, where they are preserved by baking in huge ovens.

The oil obtained from hazelnuts is inferior in flavor to that of almonds, but chemists maintain this oil is perfect as a base for several perfumes because it mixes easily and retains odors.

In England the hazel is planted for practical purposes. For instance, the wood is used for making the special charcoal from which painters and engravers get their drawing pencils. The hazel, being extremely tough and flexible, is also used for javelin shafts and for fishing poles. Hazel roots are employed by cabinet makers as material for veneering. Chips from the hazel are also used in many wine-producing countries to refine turbid wine.

IN THE BUSH

If you have gathered a lot of hazelnuts and want to remove the inner skin, this can be done very easily by spreading them in a baking pan and heating them in a 325° oven for 10 to 30 minutes. Let them cool and then the skin can be rubbed off with a towel.

An old Indian trick, which has saved me many hours of labor, is to look in hollow tree trunks where the squirrels have collected their winter's storage. In 9 out of 10 cases the squirrel has forgotten it. But a word of advice. Don't probe the hollow space with your hand because if the place is occupied, you may receive a nasty bite.

HAZELNUT CAKE

6 egg yolks	¼ cup bread crumbs
1 whole egg	6 egg whites
¾ cup sugar	1 teaspoon flour
2 cups grated hazelnuts	Filling

Preheat the oven to 225°. Using a large mixing bowl, beat the egg yolks and the whole egg with an electric beater until the mixture is thick and light yellow. Gradually beat in ½ cup of sugar, then the grated nuts and the bread crumbs. Beat until the mixture is a moist mass.

In another bowl, beat the egg whites with a wire whisk until they begin to foam. Add ¼ cup of sugar. Beat until the whites form stiff unwavering peaks. With a spatula mix about ¼ of the whites into the hazelnut mixture, then sprinkle the flour over it and gently fold in the rest of the whites.

Butter and line a 10-inch spring form pan with bread crumbs, making sure any excess is removed. Pour the batter into the form, smooth the top and bake in the middle of the oven for 45 minutes or until a skewer inserted in the middle comes out clean. Invert the cake form on 3 water glasses, and cool in an upside down position.

When the cake is cool slice in 2 equal layers, using a long serrated knife.

FILLING AND DECORATION

2 cups heavy cream, chilled	1 cup grated hazelnuts
1 teaspoon sugar	

Whip the chilled cream with an electric beater until it begins to thicken. Add the sugar and continue to beat until the cream holds its shape firmly. Take half of the whipped cream and transfer to another bowl. Fold in ¾ cup of the grated hazelnuts. Place the bottom layer of the cake on a piece of wax paper at least 18 inches square and with a spatula smooth on the cream with nuts to a thickness of about ¼ inch. Put the top layer on and using the other half of the cream, completely mask the cake top and sides. Decorate with the remaining nuts.

HAZELNUT MACAROONS

5 egg whites	½ cup all purpose flour
⅛ teaspoon salt	1 teaspoon baking powder
2 cups confectioners' sugar	3 cups grated hazelnuts

Preheat oven to 225°. In a large mixing bowl beat the egg whites and salt with an electric beater until the whites stand in peaks.

Gradually beat in the confectioners' sugar. Sift in the flour and the baking powder, then gently fold in the hazelnuts.

Grease a cookie sheet. Drop ½ tablespoons of the mixture on the sheet about 1½ inches apart. Place the sheet in the middle of the oven and bake 15 minutes or until the macaroons are lightly colored. Cool and store in a closed container.

HAZELNUT COOKIES

8 tablespoons soft butter	1 egg, lightly beaten
½ teaspoon sugar	½ teaspoon salt
1¼ cups all purpose flour	¾ cup grated hazelnuts
2 hard-cooked eggs	

Preheat oven to 350°. Using a large mixing bowl, cream the butter and sugar with an electric beater at medium speed until the mixture is fluffy and light. Beat in the flour a little at a time. Mash the hard-boiled eggs through a sieve with a wooden spoon and beat them into the mixture together with the lightly beaten egg and the salt. Beat the mixture until it forms a slightly stiff dough. Shape the dough into a ball, wrap in wax paper and refrigerate for at least 2 hours.

On a slightly floured surface roll out the dough into strips ¼ inch thick and about 6 inches wide. It should be about 15 to 16 inches long. Sprinkle the hazelnuts evenly over the surface of the dough, pressing down the nuts slightly with a rolling pin. Turn the pastry lengthwise in front of you and roll the dough up as you would a jelly roll into a long tubular shape. Wrap in a piece of wax paper and refrigerate for 1 hour.

Grease with butter two 12 by 15 inch baking sheets. Remove the roll from the refrigerator and slice crosswise into ¾-inch slices.

Arrange side by side on the cookie sheets and bake in the middle of the oven for about 15 minutes or until they have become a delicate golden color.

Cool on the cookie sheets.

135

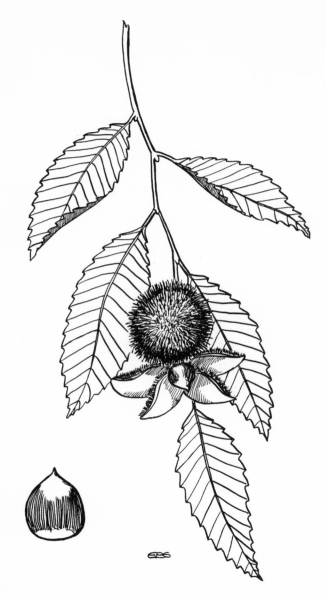

CHESTNUT

CHESTNUT

(Castanea dentata)

The chestnut is a large tree, sometimes 75 to 80 feet in height, with a trunk that usually is long and straight. It is easily distinguished from any other species by its prickly burrs which contain 1 or more shiny brown nuts.

The leaves are alternate and simple. Widest about the middle, they are coarse-toothed with sharp incurved teeth 6 to 9 inches long. In color they are a dull yellow-green above and paler beneath. The flowers are white or pinkish. The fruit is a dark brown, thin-shelled, sweet edible nut about ¾ of an inch long, found alone or in clusters of 2 to 5 in a rounded prickly burr. The bark is smooth and dark brown at first, becoming furrowed into hard scale-like ridges.

The chestnut was attacked about 40 years ago by the chestnut blight, a fungus disease introduced into North America from Asia. Fortunately a few trees survived, and the chestnut can still be found in our bush. If you are lucky enough to come across a tree, you will have a delightful meal of nuts.

IN THE BUSH

I place the nuts in the coals of my campfire and let them cook for about 10 minutes.

At home I usually fill a baking sheet with coarse salt about 1 inch thick, place the nuts in the salt, and bake in the oven for ½ hour at 350°.

They are served with butter.

WILD RICE

WILD RICE
(Zizania aquatica)

Rice is a plume-topped grass, growing from 4 to 6 feet tall, with a stout stem. The leaves are long and narrow, averaging between 1 and 3 feet long and close to 1 inch wide. The plants are tipped with long clusters of flowers that are of 2 different kinds: pollen-bearing below and seed-bearing towards the top. The seeds become dark and rodlike, expanding in husks that are stiffly tipped with a hairlike growth. This plant grows in moving water with a mucky or silty bottom.

Wild rice was a notable Indian food. Today it is considered a delicacy and is too expensive to buy regularly, but you can gather it yourself in the fall. For this purpose, the Indians used a canoe which was paddled into the stands of wild rice. The husks were bent over the canoe with the paddle, and a long stick was used to knock the seeds from the husks. The Indians let the rice fall into the bottom of the canoe, and when they had gathered a boatful, the canoe was paddled to shore and emptied. The rice was spread out on large hides to dry in the sun. (It is most important to dry wild rice thoroughly.)

To get rid of the chaff, the Indians used a two-storied contraption made out of 2 hides. After the rice was thoroughly dried, 4 poles were driven into the ground. The poles were about 6 feet tall. One hide was tied between the poles. Another was placed on the ground to one side of the first. When a brisk wind was blowing, the Indians raked the rice off the edge of the upper hide and let it fall to the hide on the ground. The loose chaff was then blown away.

The rice has a purple-black color, and the seeds have a smoky sweetness which is excellent with game and poultry. Wild rice should be thoroughly washed in cold water before using or you might have a little too much of this smoky flavor. Personally, I prefer the rather heavy taste which reminds me of slow-flowing streams and shallow lakes.

The only drawback to this delicacy is the high expense involved in using it in great quantity. But in my opinion, even if you have to buy it over the counter, the product you receive is worth nearly every penny you pay.

IN THE BUSH
BOILED RICE

Get 1½ cups of water boiling and add some salt if you have it. Add a cup of rice to the water a little at a time so the boiling never stops. Cook for 35 minutes or until you can bite easily through a test kernel. Remove from your campfire and drain. Let the pot stand close to the fire so all the steam will evaporate and the rice becomes dry.

WILD RICE CROQUETTES

If you have a stew of squirrel or bush mice boiling on the campfire, take out the bones, add 1 cup of rice to the boiling stew, and simmer on the campfire for 1 hour. Add to the pan ½ cup of cattail pollen and simmer until the stew is a heavy paste. Take the pot off the fire and cool. Using two stones, grind some cattail pollen coarsely. Take some of the stew and make a ball of it and roll in the cattail pollen. If you have some fat in your frying pan, melt this and let the balls cook in the fat until they are golden brown. If you don't have a frying pan with you, wrap the balls in green leaves and put them in the coals for 30 minutes.

FRIED WILD RICE

Start by boiling 1 cup of wild rice until tender. In the meantime, get some wild onions peeled and finely chopped. Melt some fat or margarine in a frying pan or in a piece of aluminum foil on a hot stone. Now add the onions and let them fry in the fat until they are brown. Add the rice and fry for 10 minutes. This is particularly good if you have some meat or bacon to add to the rice.

POPPED WILD RICE

Place a small quantity of your best unwashed seeds in a sieve, or whatever you can make up to look like a sieve. Melt all the fat from a porcupine. When the fat starts to smoke it is time to immerse the seeds in it until the kernels pop. Take them out of the fat and drain on spruce bows. This will take away some of the wild taste of the porcupine fat.

HOME RECIPES
WILD RICE WITH SAFFRON

2 tablespoons butter	3 cups boiling water
2 tablespoons finely chopped wild onions	¼ teaspoon ground saffron
1½ cups wild rice	1½ teaspoons salt

In a 2 to 3-quart saucepan, melt the butter over high heat. When it gives off a nutty odor, lower the heat and add the wild onions. Cook for 6 minutes or until the onions are golden brown. Pour in the rice and stirring well, coat the grains with butter. Do not let the rice brown.

Add the ground saffron to 1 cup of boiling water and mix well. Stir into the pan, making sure all the rice is coated. Add the rest of the water and the salt, and bring to a boil, stirring constantly. Lower the heat to a slow simmer and cover the pan tightly. Cook undisturbed for 35 minutes or until all the moisture is gone and the rice grains are tender but not too soft. Before serving the rice, fluff it up with a fork and taste for seasoning.

WILD RICE PUDDING

2 tablespoons anise seed	1 cup wild rice
1 tablespoon ginger root	¼ teaspoon salt
1 cup milk	3 egg yolks
1 2-inch piece of cinnamon stick	½ cup sugar
6 cups water	1 teaspoon ground cinnamon

Wrap the ginger and the anise seed in a piece of cheesecloth. In a 2-quart saucepan, bring the milk, the cinnamon stick and the bag of spices to a boil over moderate heat. Watch the milk so it will not boil over. When the milk starts to bubble, lower the heat and cover the pan. Simmer over very low heat for 3 to 4 minutes. Remove from heat and set aside to steep for 30 to 35 minutes.

Bring 6 cups of water to a boil in a heavy 2-quart saucepan. Pour in the rice in a slow stream so the boiling never stops. Add the salt, reduce the heat and cook uncovered for 35 minutes. Drain the rice through a large sieve and place the sieve in a saucepan over low heat to let the rice dry. Stir with a fork to separate the grains.

Using a large mixing bowl, beat the egg yolks and sugar together with a rotary beater until light and fluffy. Beating all the time, add the flavored milk in a thin stream.

Return the mixture to the saucepan and cook over low heat, stirring constantly with a wooden spoon until the custard starts to thicken enough to coat the spoon. Never let the mixture come to a boil at any time, as the custard will curdle. Remove the cinnamon stick and the bag with spices. Add the rice to the custard and cook over low heat for at least 5 minutes, stirring constantly with a fork. Pour the pudding into a large casserole about 8 by 12 inches and let cool. Just before serving sprinkle with ground cinnamon.

WILD RICE AND LIVER CASSEROLE

1 cup wild rice	2 tablespoons dark corn syrup
2 tablespoons butter	2 teaspoons salt
2 wild onions, finely chopped	¼ teaspoon pepper
2 cups milk	¼ teaspoon ground cloves
2 eggs	1½ pounds calves' liver, minced
4 slices bacon, fried crisply and	raw
crumbled	1 tablespoon butter

In a 3 to 4-quart heavy saucepan, bring 3 quarts of water to a boil. Add a teaspoon salt, and slowly pour in the rice without disturbing the boiling water.

Remove from the heat after 20 minutes and drain thoroughly, using a large sieve. Let the rice dry in the sieve in a saucepan over low heat, stirring with a fork to separate the kernels. Set aside.

In a heavy 10-inch skillet, melt the butter over high heat. When it gives off a nutty odor, lower the heat and add the finely chopped onions. Cook for 5 to 6 minutes over moderate heat until the onions are soft and transparent. Remove from heat and set aside.

Preheat the oven to 375°. In a large mixing bowl gently combine the rice and the milk, the eggs, corn syrup, crumbled bacon, onions and the seasonings. Stir in the minced liver and mix thoroughly.

With a pastry brush spread the remaining butter on the bottom and sides of a 2-quart casserole. Pour in the liver-rice mixture. Bake in the oven on the middle shelf for 1 to 1½ hours or until a knife inserted in the middle comes out clean. Serve hot with cranberry sauce and potatoes.

WILD RICE WINE

3 **pounds wild rice**	1 **lemon**
3 **pounds sugar**	1 **ounce cherry wine yeast**
1 **gallon warm water**	**Pinch of isinglass (clearing**
1 **pound large raisins**	**agent)**

Put the rice and sugar in a large bowl and cover with the warm water. Put the raisins through a meat grinder and add to the rice-sugar mixture. Then squeeze into it the juice from the lemon. Making sure the temperature of the water is not over 65°, sprinkle the yeast and the isinglass on top. Cover and let ferment for 9 days, stirring often the first 3 days. After 9 days, strain through a fine sieve lined with a paper filter.

Put the liquid into gallon fermenting jars. Instal fermentation locks and let stand. Bottle the wine when it is completely clear.

This wine is strong and harsh at first but improves greatly with age. I use this wine mainly to prepare Japanese rice dishes.

BRAISED WILD RICE WITH CRAWFISH

3 **quarts cold water**	2 **wild onions**
¼ **cup coarse salt**	2 **sprigs parsley**
3 **large bunches fresh dill**	1 **bay leaf**
20 **live freshwater crawfish**	5 **tablespoons butter**
2 **pounds fish trimmings**	2 **cups wild rice**
2 **quarts water**	4 **tablespoons soft butter**
1 **cup dry white wine**	½ **cup cheese**

In a 6-quart kettle combine the cold water and salt. Bring to a boil over high heat. Add 2 bunches of dill and boil briskly for 10 minutes. Wash the crawfish under cold running water. Drop into the boiling water a few at a time, making sure that the boiling never stops. When all the crawfish have been added, cover the kettle and boil for 10 minutes. Line a 3 to 4-quart mixing bowl with a bunch of dill. Remove the crawfish from the kettle and place on top of the dill. Strain the stock from the kettle through a large sieve into the bowl with the crawfish. Cool to room temperature. Refrigerate for at least 24 hours.

Drain the crawfish and discard the stock and dill. Shell the crawfish carefully and save the shells. With a small knife slit the crawfish down the back and lift out the black intestinal vein. With a small hammer break the claws and remove the meat. Wash all the meat under cold running water and dry it on paper towels.

In a 3 to 4-quart enamel saucepan, combine the fish trimmings and the trimmings and shells from the crawfish, the water and wine. Bring to a boil over high heat, removing the scum as it rises in the pan. Add the onions, parsley and bay leaf. Reduce the heat and simmer for 30 minutes. Strain the stock through a fine sieve into another saucepan. Discard the fish trimmings and shells of the crawfish. Set the pot of strained stock over low heat and let it barely simmer.

Using a heavy 10-inch skillet, melt 1 tablespoon of butter over high heat. When it gives off a nutty odor, reduce the heat, add the crawfish and cook for 4 to 5 minutes, stirring constantly. Cover and set aside.

Melt 4 tablespoons of butter in a 3-quart flameproof casserole. Add the wild rice and cook over moderate heat for 5 to 6 minutes, stirring constantly. Add 2 cups of the simmering stock and cook until it is absorbed by the rice. Add another 2 cups of the stock and cook until this has been absorbed. Check that the rice is tender. If not, add ½ cup of stock and cook until it is very tender.

With a fish fork gently stir in the crawfish, the juice from the skillet and the soft butter. Sprinkle the cheese over the top of the casserole and stir gently into the mixture.

It is important at this time to stir very gently so you do not break up the crawfish pieces.

STEAMED WILD RICE

2 cups wild rice	3 cups water

Pour the rice into a sieve and hold under cold running water. Stir with a fork and let the water run until it is clear. The washing is necessary to remove some of the smoky taste from the rice.

Put a flameproof bowl upside down on the bottom of a large kettle and place a deep plate right side up on top of the bowl. Add 3 cups of water, or more if the kettle is very large.

Place the rice on the plate and put the kettle over high heat. When the water boils, cover the kettle and boil for 20 minutes. Remove from the heat and let the rice rest covered in the kettle for 5 more minutes. Uncover and stir the rice to separate the grains. Serve at once.

WILD RICE AND RABBIT CASSEROLE

1 cup cattail seeds	1 small bay leaf
1½ cups wild rice	5 or 6 whole cloves
2 quarts water	½ teaspoon salt
6 tablespoons butter	¼ teaspoon pepper
1 cup finely chopped wild onions	½ pound pepperoni
2 to 2½ pounds rabbit	½ cup water
Salt and pepper	4 eggs, beaten

Crush the cattail seeds between two pieces of wax paper with a rolling pin or a bottle. Place the rice and the seeds in a 3 to 4-quart saucepan and add the water. Bring to a boil over high heat, reduce heat and simmer for 30 minutes.

In a heavy 12-inch skillet, melt the butter over high heat and when it gives off a nutty odor, lower the heat and add the onions. Cook for 5 minutes or until the onions are golden brown. Remove the onions with a slotted spoon and set aside.

Cut the rabbit into 8 serving pieces. Pat the pieces dry with a paper towel and sprinkle with salt and pepper. Add the rabbit to the skillet and brown well over high heat.

Turn the pieces of rabbit with tongs and regulate the heat so they brown on all sides without burning. When they are nicely brown, transfer to a plate.

When the cattail seeds and rice have simmered for 30 minutes, add the onions, rabbit, bay leaf, cloves and the salt and pepper. Cover tightly and simmer for 45 minutes.

In a 10-inch skillet, melt ½ tablespoon butter over high heat. Reduce heat when butter gives off a nutty aroma. Cut the pepperoni in 1-inch lengths, add to the skillet with the water and cook for 10 minutes, then add it to the rabbit and rice mixture.

Preheat the oven to 400°. Grease an 8 by 8 by 3-inch casserole lightly with butter. Pour all the ingredients from the saucepan into the casserole after removing the bay leaf and cloves.

Level the top of the stew and pour the beaten eggs over the ingredients. Place the casserole in the oven uncovered, and bake for 10 minutes or until the eggs are firm and lightly browned.

Serve at once.

WILD RICE WITH BRAISED VEAL

2 tablespoons butter	1 teaspoon salt
8 slices bacon, cut in ¼-inch pieces	½ teaspoon pepper
	1 cup wild onions, finely chopped
2 pounds boneless veal, cut into 1½-inch cubes	1 cup beef stock
	1½ cups wild rice

Preheat the oven to 375°. In a 12-inch skillet, melt the butter over high heat until it gives off a nutty odor. Reduce heat and fry bacon until it is crisp and golden brown on all sides. Remove with a slotted spoon and set aside to drain on paper towels.

Pat the veal cubes dry, then brown them in the skillet over medium heat. As they brown transfer them to a 2 to 3-quart casserole and sprinkle with the salt and pepper.

Pour the fat from the skillet and save. Leave a thin film in the bottom of the skillet and fry the onions for 8 minutes until they are golden brown. Add the beef stock to the skillet and bring to a boil, stirring in all the browned bits from the bottom and sides. Pour the stock and onions over the veal cubes in the casserole and bring to a boil on top of the stove. Then cover tightly and place in the oven to bake for 45 minutes.

Wash the wild rice under cold running water and drain. Add the rice and bacon to the casserole and return the dish to the oven to bake for another 45 minutes. Stir with a fork once or twice during this time. Do not let cook dry. If necessary, add 1 or 2 tablespoons of beef stock to keep mixture moist.

If you wish, you can sprinkle some grated cheese on top of the casserole before serving.

DEEP-FRIED WILD RICE AND CHEESE BALLS

1 quart water	1 cup grated mild cheese
2 cups wild rice	1 cup dry bread crumbs
2 eggs	Vegetable oil for deep-frying

In a 2-quart saucepan bring the water to a boil over high heat and add the washed wild rice in a slow stream so that the water never stops boiling. Stir once or twice, reduce the heat to a slow simmer and cover the pan. Simmer for 35 minutes. Take off the heat and drain through a sieve. Empty the pot of water and place the sieve over the pot to let the rice dry thoroughly. In a large mixing bowl beat the eggs lightly with an electric beater. Add the rice and stir with a fork, making sure not to mash it. Set aside.

Cut the cheese in ½-inch cubes. Scoop up a tablespoon of the mixture and place a cheese cube in the middle. Using another spoon, take a second spoonful of the mixture and place on top of the first. Press the two spoons together and form a ball. I prefer to do this operation with my hands.

Roll the balls in bread crumbs and put them on a platter covered with wax paper. When all the mixture is used, place the platter in the refrigerator and let stand for 45 minutes.

Heat the oil in a deep fat fryer to 375°. Preheat the oven to 250°. Line a large baking dish with paper towels and put the dish in the oven.

Fry the balls 6 or 7 at a time for 8 minutes or until they are golden brown and the cheese has melted. With a slotted spoon transfer the balls from the fryer to the dish in the oven to drain.

Serve at once with cranberry jelly as a complement.

CHOKECHERRY

146

CHOKECHERRY

(Prunus virginiana)

The chokecherry is a large shrub or a small tree native to North America. It is thicket forming and is found in open woods but more often seen on stream banks or on rocky sites. The leaves are from 2 to 4 inches long and about half as wide, oval with abrupt points. They are smooth and thin, dull green above and paler below. Their edges are finely indented with narrowly pointed teeth. The long clusters of flowers blossom when the leaves are nearly grown. The fruit is a red to black berry the size of a pea.

Unlike the rum cherry, the wood of the chokecherry has no commercial value, but the structure of the tree is the same as the rum cherry.

This native shrub is found throughout the continent from the far north to the far south. Old recipes from frontier days indicate that it played an important part in the early settler's diet.

IN THE BUSH

It is a tedious job to stone this small fruit, but you will forget all your troubles when it appears on the table as a **complement to roast venison.**

I will never forget a visit to a small trapper's cabin in the northern part of Canada during a howling blizzard. The open fireplace was blazing, and the smell of venison from the great iron pot was irresistible. When the old Indian trapper finally put the roast on the table, accompanied by a fine chokecherry jelly, it was a feast fit for a king. The roast was eaten to the accompaniment of old Indian tales, and the fire was burning low before we got to bed, full of tales and meat.

Many a summer afternoon, after a hot fishing trip, I have sat by a stand of chokecherry trees to get refreshment from the small berries. The limbs of the chokecherry are often so laden with fruit that the branches bend under the weight. The berries are rich in vitamins and are an excellent **survival food,** as they can be eaten raw when travelling.

HOME RECIPES
CHOKECHERRY CAKE

4 eggs	¼ cup sugar
1½ cups milk	3 cups fresh chokecherries, pitted
½ cup flour	Confectioners' sugar

Preheat the oven to 375°. Break the eggs into a large mixing bowl, add milk and mix with an electric beater. Add the flour a little at a time, then the sugar. Mix well until you have a smooth creamy batter.

Pit the cherries and wash under cold running water. Pat dry with paper towels. Grease a 6-cup baking dish with butter and spread the cherries on the bottom evenly.

Pour in the batter and bake in the middle of the oven for 1½ hours or until the top is golden brown and firm to touch.

Dust lightly with confectioners' sugar and serve warm with vanilla sauce.

VANILLA SAUCE

¼ cup sugar	2 egg yolks
1 tablespoon cornstarch	2 cups light cream
¼ teaspoon salt	1 teaspoon vanilla

Using a 1½ to 2-quart stainless steel saucepan, mix sugar, cornstarch and salt, and put the pan on low heat. In a large mixing bowl beat the egg yolks and cream together. Pour slowly into the sugar mixture, stirring constantly. Continue to whisk and cook over low heat until the sauce is smooth and creamy, but don't let it boil.

Remove pan from the heat and stir in the vanilla. Transfer the sauce to a bowl and let cool. Cover and chill in refrigerator.

This sauce can also be served warm.

COLD SOUR CHOKECHERRY SOUP

3 cups cold water	1 tablespoon arrowroot
1 cup sugar	¼ cup heavy cream
1 cinnamon stick	1 cup dry red wine
4 cups pitted chokecherries	

Using a 2 to 3-quart saucepan, combine the water, sugar and cinnamon stick. Put over high heat and bring to a boil, then add the washed chokecherries. Cover and simmer for 45 minutes. Discard the cinnamon stick.

Mix the arrowroot into a paste with 3 tablespoons water, then slowly add the paste to the cherry soup, stirring constantly. Bring the soup to a boil and reduce heat to simmer until the soup clears and thickens.

Remove from heat and put in a bowl in refrigerator. After it is well chilled, stir in the cream and chilled wine.

Serve in chilled soup bowls with 5 or 6 cherries on top.

COLD BUTTERMILK AND CHOKECHERRY SOUP

3 cups chokecherries	1 quart buttermilk
3 egg yolks	½ cup whipped cream
½ cup sugar	

Clean and pit chokecherries, wash under cold running water and pat dry with paper towels. Using a large mixing bowl, beat the egg yolks lightly. Add sugar and beat until the mixture is smooth and thick. Slowly beat in buttermilk until the soup is creamy. With a rubber spatula fold in the cherries. Mix well but do not overmix.

Serve the soup in chilled bowls with a spoonful of whipped cream floating on top.

ELDERBERRY

(Sambucus canadensis)

You will find the elderberry along fences, banks and streams, and in the field. It is a shrub or small tree that is characterized by opposite pinnate leaves, small white flowers usually in compound cymes and the black berries. The pith in the branches is white when young, and the core of the trunk is soft and easily removable. It grows smaller with maturity. The stems often spring in erect groups from tangled roots.

ELDERBERRY

If you once have enjoyed an old-style elderberry pie, then you are on a steady hunt for these small berries. The flowers as well as the berries are edible, but even when the berries are fully ripe, they are not very palatable when fresh. But let them dry on trays in the sun or in the oven, and you will experience a change of flavor you never expected. I usually collect all the elderberries I can get my hands on in late July, and let the sun do the work of drying for me. It seems to me that elderberries dried in the sun give sweeter fruit than berries dried in the oven.

The Indians know the elderberry as "the tree of music" because many of the wind instruments that were used in their religious or ceremonial dances were made of the straight stems. The stems were cut in the spring and dried in the summer, and then the soft pith was poked out with hot sticks.

IN THE BUSH

I use the elderberry stems to make tubes for tapping maples, birches and other trees that have a tasty sap.

When in the bush in late summer I always sweeten my pancakes, waffles and muffins with this delightful fruit. **A simple way to make pancakes** is to crack 2 eggs into a tin can, put in 2 cups of flour, a couple of teaspoons of baking powder and a little sugar. Mix it all together with a cup of milk and you have a dough for pancakes. A couple of handfuls of elderberries complete the pancakes. If the pancakes then are baked on hot stones, you will have a delightful breakfast.

Early in the summer I usually make a light wine of the flowers and when the berries are ripe, the late elderberry wine is made. The colour of the wine made from the berries is just out of this world — a deep ruby red.

HOME RECIPES

ELDERBERRY JELLY

4 quarts fresh elderberries	6 cups superfine sugar
6 cups water	

Pick over the berries and remove all the stems and leaves. Do not worry if you have a lot of underripe berries because these have more pectin, the substance that causes the fruit to jell. Wash the elderberries in a colander under running water, then drop them into an 8 to 10-quart kettle. Add the 6 cups water and bring to a boil over high heat. Reduce the heat to moderate and cook uncovered for 45 minutes, stirring from time to time. Place a large sieve over a large pot, line the colander with double cheesecloth and pour in the elderberries. Allow the juice to drain into the pot without disturbing.

When the juice has drained through completely, measure it and return to the pot. Discard the elderberries. Add 1½ cups sugar for each cup of juice and bring to a boil over high heat, stirring until the sugar dissolves. Boil uncovered until the jelly reaches 220° on a candy thermometer.

Remove the pot from the heat and skim off the surface foam. Pour into hot, clean jelly glasses, and seal with ⅛ inch of melted paraffin.

JACK DAVIS ELDERBERRY WINE

18 ounces dried elderberries	2 Campden tablets
15 ounces raisins	2 teaspoons yeast nutrient
5 pounds sugar	2 gallons water
2 tablespoons citric acid	1 package wine yeast

Mix all the ingredients except the wine yeast and water in a primary fermenter (I use a plastic garbage container with lid). Boil the water and pour over the mixture in the fermenter.

Mix well and make sure the sugar is dissolved, cover with the lid and stand overnight in a room where the temperature will not go below 65° or above 70°.

Next morning sprinkle the yeast on the surface and let stand for 24 hours. Ferment in primary fermenter 6 or 7 days, stirring the ferment twice a day. On the fifth day add 1 cup sugar solution (2 parts sugar to 1 part water), let stand for 2 days and add another cup sugar solution. Let stand for 2 days, then strain the ferment through a fine sieve lined with a double layer of cheesecloth.

Let stand overnight. Siphon into 1-gallon jugs, place fermentation locks on the jugs, leave for 3 weeks and then rack into clean gallon jugs. Let stand for 3 months, rack again into clean gallon jugs, and let stand until the wine is clear and stable. Add 3 Wine-Art stabilizer tablets per gallon and rack into wine bottles.

This wine is my friend Jack's prize possession and one of the best wines I have ever tasted. It surpasses many a commercially made wine.

If you don't have any luck with this wine, don't blame Jack but me, who cannot pass on Jack's wine-making thumb.

ELDERBERRY PIE

4 tablespoons butter	4 cups elderberries
2 tablespoons flour	2 cups sugar
½ cup water	Pastry

In a heavy 2-quart saucepan melt the butter over high heat. When it gives off a nutty odor, lower the heat and add the flour, stirring constantly. Add the water and the elderberries, mix well and simmer for 5 minutes. Add the sugar and mix well. Simmer for 15 minutes or until the stew is thick and smooth. Remove from heat and set aside.

PASTRY

6 tablespoons butter	¼ teaspoon salt
2 tablespoons lard	1 tablespoon sugar
1½ cups all-purpose flour	4 tablespoons water

In a large mixing bowl combine the butter, lard, flour, salt and sugar. Using your fingertips, mix the ingredients until you have a coarse meal. Pour 3 tablespoons water over the mixture, toss lightly, and gather the dough into a ball. If the dough is too crisp and crumbles, add another tablespoon water. Dust the pastry with a little flour, wrap in wax paper and refrigerate for at least 2 hours before using.

Preheat the oven to 375°. On a lightly floured pastry board roll out half the dough in a circle ¼ inch thick. Grease a 9-inch pie plate with a little butter. Place the dough on top and press down in the middle. Form the pie crust to the plate and cut around the edges, leaving a ½ inch to be folded back to double the edge. Fill the crust with the elderberry stew. Roll out the rest of the pastry, cut in inch-wide strips and crisscross on top. Bake for 25 minutes.

RASPBERRY

RASPBERRY

(Rubus idaeus, Rubus occidentalis)

Rubus idaeus and *rubus occidentalis* are the two most common raspberries. Rubus idaeus has canes that are erect, not rooting at the tip. The leaves are pale and soft, pubescent on the under surface, and the fruit is red. In *Rubus occidentalis* the canes arch and root at the tip. The prickles are broad at the base, stout and curved. The fruit is purple or black.

The experts have trouble identifying the differences in the many members of the raspberry and blackberry family. As a matter of fact, they cannot agree on how many varieties we have in the United States and Canada.

But does this really matter? Anyone who has come upon a clearing where a forest fire has gone through a couple of years previously and has seen and tasted these magnificent red or black berries is not going to be worried over technicalities when he has gallon after gallon of fruit at his fingertips. The high vitamin C content makes the berries a wonderful survival food, particularly since they are easily recognized by everyone. The wild varieties of raspberry are, in general, of the same appearance as the market varieties.

The early settlers made an excellent **diarrhea remedy** out of blackberries. They used 4 quarts of blackberries boiled in 1 quart of water until mushy and then strained. For every quart of juice, stir in 2 cups of sugar. Then tie 1 tablespoon of cloves, 1 tablespoon of cinnamon and 1 tablespoon of allspice in a piece of cheesecloth. Drop this bag into the juice, boil for 30 minutes and let cool. Add one pint of whiskey to every quart of syrup. Pour into clean bottles and cork securely.

To Freeze: If you wish to conserve this delightful fruit and have a freezer, it is an easy task. Use 1 pound of sugar to 4 pounds of fruit. Mix the sugar into the berries very gently without crushing the berries. Pack into freezer bags and freeze as soon as you can. I find the easiest way to mix in the sugar is to spread the berries on a large piece of wax paper and sprinkle the sugar on top. Then, with a large metal spatula gently put the berries into the bags.

IN THE BUSH

The tender, young, peeled shoots and twigs are edible and somehow pleasant to chew on.

As Tea: The leaves make an excellent tea, either steeped in boiling water or taken home and dried in the sun and used as you would any commercial tea.

HOME RECIPES

FROZEN WILD RASPBERRY JAM

3 cups crushed wild raspberries	2 tablespoons lemon juice
5 cups superfine sugar	½ bottle liquid pectin

Pick the berries over and remove any small white worms or badly bruised fruit. In a 2 or 3-quart stainless steel kettle crush the berries and add the sugar and lemon juice. Let stand for at least ½ hour, stirring from time to time. Add the liquid pectin (or 1 package pectin crystals in ¾ cup of water — the water has to be boiling when you add the crystals, but you let it cool before adding to the raspberries.)

Blend the mixture well and let stand overnight at room temperature. Pour into freezer cartons or freezer bags. If you are using bags, make sure they are securely tied. Place in freezer.

WILD RASPBERRY JAM

8 cups crushed wild raspberries	6 cups superfine sugar

Clean the berries by immersing them in a large sieve into cold water. Pick them over well and remove any that contain white worms.

Using a 3 to 4-quart enamel or stainless steel saucepan, crush the berries, put the pan over medium heat and heat thoroughly. When the berries are hot, add the sugar, stirring constantly to make sure all the sugar is dissolved.

Cook the mixture until it reaches a thick, jelly-like consistency. Pour into sterilized jars and seal with melted paraffin.

To Sterilize Jars: Wash and rinse jars or jelly glasses. Invert in a shallow pan. Set the pan in a preheated oven at 275°. Add water to about 1 inch depth. Let stand in the oven for at least 15 minutes. Remove and turn jars right side up, one at a time, as you use them.

To Seal with Paraffin: It is a high fire hazard to melt paraffin if you don't take a few precautionary steps. Place the paraffin block in a small saucepan and stand this pan in a larger pan filled with boiling water. Let the paraffin melt. When pouring the paraffin, make sure you are well away from the stove so no spilling will land on a hot element. Only ⅛ of an inch thickness of paraffin is needed to preserve the jam.

WILD RASPBERRY BREAD PUDDING

2 quarts wild raspberries	12 slices homemade style white
2 cups superfine sugar	bread
	2 cups heavy cream

Pick over the wild raspberries carefully, removing any that contain a worm or are badly bruised. Wash in a large sieve under cold running water.

Shake the berries dry. Place in a large mixing bowl and sprinkle the sugar on top. Toss the berries very gently with a large spoon until all the sugar has dissolved. Cover the berries and set aside.

Cut a slice of bread to fit the bottom of a deep 2-quart bowl. Trim 8 or 9 slices of bread into wedges about 4 inches at the top and 3 inches across the bottom. Line the sides of the bowl with the wedges, overlapping each one by about a ½ inch. Pour the fruit into the bowl and cover the top completely with the rest of the bread. Cover the top of the bowl with a flat plate and place a weight on top of the plate. Place in the refrigerator for at least 12 hours.

Remove the mold by placing a chilled serving plate upside down on the bowl, and quickly inverting it. The mold should slide out easily.

Whip the cream in a large chilled bowl until it holds its shape. With a rubber spatula cover the mold on the outside and top. Using a cake decorator set, decorate with curls and roses. Serve chilled.

RASPBERRY TEA

Collect several bags of raspberry leaves. Spread them on newspapers and dry outside in the sun for 4 days. Place the partly dried leaves in a baking pan and leave overnight in a 200° oven. Put the dried leaves into sealed containers and you will have a good tea for the winter.

To make the tea, pour hot water into the teapot and let stand for 10 minutes. Boil a kettle full of water. Discard the water in the teapot. Place 5 or 6 dried and crumbled raspberry leaves in the pot and fill with the boiling water. Let steep for 5 minutes and serve with milk and sugar.

RASPBERRYADE

Pick the berries over and discard any badly bruised ones. Pack into jars and fill in the spaces with white vinegar. Seal the jars and let stand for a month. Strain off the juices through a fine sieve lined with a double layer of cheesecloth, and put away in sterilized jars or bottles.

To serve, sweeten to taste with fine sugar and dilute with ice water.

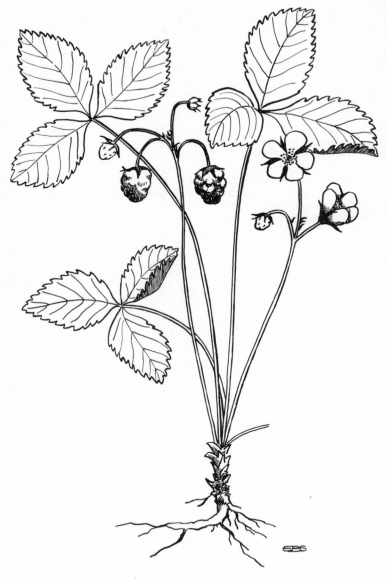

STRAWBERRY

STRAWBERRY

(Fragaria)

The leaves of the wild strawberry are dark. The flowers are white and berries are dark red with pitted skin. The stems of the plant often trail out and produce new roots. The plant grows along stream banks and in open fields.

Not too many plants, if any, will give you sweeter fruit than the strawberry. Very few wild fruits are so rich in calories as strawberries.

Also, wild strawberries have twice as much vitamin A as canned pineapple and 3 times as much as grapefruit. They also have a large amount of vitamin C — only a quarter cup of berries contains as much vitamin C as an orange.

When I was a child, we used to pick strawberries and thread them on a straw like a string of pearls. I still find myself doing this if I run across a strawberry patch without anything to carry the berries in.

It is a great feast for both the eyes and the taste buds to find a colony of strawberries in the bush and just sit down and eat as much as your stomach can hold.

IN THE BUSH

As you know, the berries can be eaten raw, cooked, mashed or any way you can think of.

As Tea: A refreshing tea can be made of the leaves from the strawberry plant. Just pick a handful of leaves and pour 2 cups of boiling water over them to steep for 5 minutes.

As a Beverage: A cool drink can be made by crushing a handful of berries and adding them to a glass of cold, fresh spring water. A half teaspoon of sugar will really bring out the flavor.

Recipes for strawberries are counted in the thousands, but here are a few which I like particularly.

HOME RECIPES
STRAWBERRY PIE

3 cups flour	5 tablespoons ice water
1 cup lard	1 tablespoon vinegar
1 teaspoon salt	Strawberry filling
1 egg	

Preheat oven to 400°. Using a large mixing bowl, sift the flour into the bowl and add the lard and the salt. Using your fingertips, mix the ingredients until you have a flaky texture. Add the egg, ice water and vinegar. Mix all together until the texture is very fine and all crumbs have disappeared. Form the dough into a ball, wrap in wax paper and refrigerate for at least 1 hour.

Remove from refrigerator and roll out the dough on a slightly floured pastry board. Roll to ¼-inch thickness. Invert a 9-inch pie plate over the dough and cut around it 2 inches out from the edge to get dough that will fit the plate.

Grease the pie plate and place the dough in the plate, then bake for 15 minutes.

STRAWBERRY FILLING

1 cup fresh strawberries, crushed	1 cup water
½ cup sugar	Strawberries
2 tablespoons cornstarch	

Pour the crushed strawberries and sugar into a 2-quart saucepan and place over low heat. Add the water with the cornstarch mixed into it. Cook until thick and syrupy. Pack the cooked piecrust full of ripe juicy strawberries and when the syrup is ready, pour it over the berries in the crust. Cool and serve.

STRAWBERRY PUDDING

¼ pound butter	6 egg whites
¼ cup sugar	1 teaspoon baking soda dissolved
6 egg yolks	in 2 tablespoons milk
1 cup all purpose flour	1 cup fresh strawberries
2 cups fresh strawberries	¼ cup sugar

Coat the bottom and sides of a plain quart mold with a tablespoon of butter.

Using a large mixing bowl, cream the butter and sugar together until they are light and fluffy. Beat in the egg yolks one at a time. Beat in the flour, making sure all the ingredients are well mixed. With a rubber spatula fold in the strawberries, being careful not to mash them to mush.

Using an electric beater, beat the egg whites until they form unwavering peaks when the beaters are lifted out of the bowl. Quickly stir the baking soda and milk into the batter and then gently fold in the egg whites.

Pour this mixture into the mold and cover tightly with aluminum foil. Place the mold in a roasting pan and fill it with water to halfway up the sides of the mold. Bring the water to a boil over high heat, cover the roast pan tightly, reduce heat and simmer for 2 hours.

Remove the mold from the pan and let rest for a minute or so. Remove the foil, place a pie plate on top of the mold and quickly turn them over. The pudding should slide out easily.

Crush the cup of strawberries, stir in the sugar and let stand for 10 minutes.

Pour over the pudding just before you serve it.

STRAWBERRY LEAVES TEA

Collect leaves from the strawberry plants in late summer. Place on paper in the sun to dry for several days. Remember to take the leaves inside before the sun sets, as the dew will moisten them and you will have to start all over again.

After a week in the sun, I usually put them on a cookie sheet in a 125° oven overnight.

Crumble the leaves and put them in an airtight container. This will give you a dandy cold remedy all winter long, or so I believe because if I have a cup of strawberry tea every day, I don't seem to pick up a cold. Try it and let me know.

WILD ROSE

(Rosa)

Some thirty-five or more varieties of wild roses are found around the United States and Canada. The wild rose grows in thickets. Its flowers are soft, delicate, five-petaled, and pink or light red in color. The plant is usually thorny.

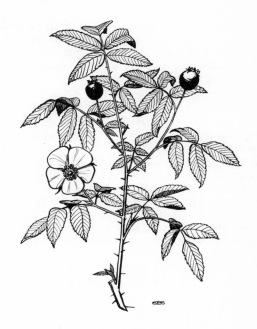

WILD ROSE

The fruit, or rose hip, has one of the richest vitamin contents of all our wild edibles. The juice is twenty-five times richer in vitamin C than orange juice.

The rose hip is an important survival food because you can easily recognize this plant, and the chances you will get the wrong plant are almost nonexistent. Usually you can pick the fruit all year round. I have picked rose hips at temperatures as low as 50° below zero.

During the war rose hips were an important source of vitamins in the Scandinavian countries when all import of citrus fruits was cut off by the German blockade. Millions of pounds of rose hips were gathered every year, and the uses were as many as you can think of. We used the dried fruit in soups, hot and cold drinks, and in many more ways. In the Swedish Air Force survival school we taught our students to carry a handful of rose hips in their pockets and eat them as a stimulant when under heavy physical strain.

IN THE BUSH

An easy way to dry this excellent fruit is to place handfuls in a kettle and hang the kettle over a slow fire or set it in the coals of the campfire. In the morning you have a bundle of nicely dried rose hips.

As a Sugar Substitute: Many people discard the seeds, but the seeds contain a lot of vitamin E. Save the seeds, grind them, boil in a small amount of water, and strain through a cheesecloth, and you can use the syrup as a substitute for any syrup called for in recipes.

As Tea: Even the flowers are useful as a rather tasty tea. Many a time I have enjoyed a cup of rose tea in the bush. This tea sweetened with a little wild honey is a delightful drink for a tired and thirsty woodsman.

It seems that dark red roses are stronger tasting and the flavor becomes more delicate as the colors lighten.

HOME RECIPES

ROSE HIP JELLY

| 6 cups rose hips | ½ bottle liquid pectin |
| 2 cups water | 4 cups superfine sugar |

Snip the bud ends of the rose hips. Coarsely grind or mince them. Place the pulp in a 2 or 3-quart saucepan and add the water. Place over low heat and simmer for 1 hour or until the pulp is very tender.

Strain through a jelly bag of cheesecloth, pressing down on the fruit with a wooden spoon. Clean the pot and measure into it 3 cups of the juice and 4 cups of sugar. Bring to a boil, stirring constantly, and add the fruit pectin. Boil for 4 minutes, stirring all the time. Remove from heat and skim the surface.

Pour into sterilized jelly jars and seal with paraffin.

ROSE HIP PURÉE

| 1 pound rose hips | 3 cups of water |

Snip the bud ends of the rose hips with a sharp knife. Coarsely grind or mince the hips. Place the hips in a 3-quart stainless steel saucepan with the water, bring to a boil over high heat, lower the heat and simmer for 30 minutes.

Place a fine sieve over a large mixing bowl and press the rose hips through the sieve to make a stiff purée. Add enough water to make 4 cups of purée. Pour the purée into sterilized jars and seal with paraffin. Store in a cold place. Use as a sugar substitute.

ROSE HIP SOUP

1 cup rose hip purée	2 tablespoons sugar
1 cup water	Heavy cream

This soup is a very popular Scandinavian dessert. It is customarily served chilled, with whipped cream.

Add the water and sugar to the rose hip purée. Heat in a saucepan, stirring constantly.

Remove from heat, pour into individual serving bowls and place in the refrigerator.

Just before serving put 2 tablespoons of whipped cream on each dessert.

ROSE HIP MEAL

Collect the rose hips when they are ripe. Sun dry for a couple of days, then bring inside and let them dry for a couple of weeks. When the rose hips are completely dry, crush them and using a food mill or blender, pulverize them to a fine powder. Place the powder in an airtight container. When you use the powder, remember it is full strength and a tablespoon is equal to a cup of freshly picked rose hips.

ROSE FLOWER TEA

The flowers can be gathered and dried and made into tea. It is very simple. Use 2 tablespoons dried rose flowers, cover them with boiling water, steep the tea for 5 minutes. A little honey or sugar will help to bring out the fragrance.

BLACK BIRCH

BLACK BIRCH

(Betula lenta)

This tree is easily identified by its reddish-brown bark, which has the aroma of the wintergreen. The leaves are a dull green on the upper side and pale green or yellow on the under side. They are from 2 to 3 inches long and oval, with double-toothed edges.

The bark of the black birch is often used as a substitute for the wintergreen plant in producing the fragrant wintergreen oils. Indians used to make a drink of the finely ground bark, and in districts where no sugar maple was found, the sap from the birch was used instead to produce syrup and a sugar substitute.

IN THE BUSH

The sap is delightful right from the tree, boiled down or fresh. A unique method of caloric intake was demonstrated to me by an old Indian guide who was teaching me the rudiments of survival.

One day we had been traveling through rough terrain, and all my energy was exhausted when he finally saw fit to call a halt. He started to set the campfire and asked me what I wanted for supper. I told him I didn't care for supper, just rest and sleep. He then wondered how I would like to eat and sleep at the same time. I thought this an excellent idea, but how could it be done? My friend cut me a hollow straw about 12 inches long and then cut a slit in the nearest black birch tree just high enough from the ground so that when I was lying down with a root as a pillow, the straw would reach the corner of my mouth. Very soon the sap started gently to drop into my mouth, but a dreadful thought entered by mind. Asleep, how would I know when I had had enough food? "Don't you worry," he said. "When your stomach is full you will turn, and the straw will fall out of the tree or your mouth." Sure enough, tired as I was I soon fell asleep and I didn't know a thing before morning when I was awakened by the smoke from the campfire. The old Indian said, "Did you have a good sleep and are you hungry?" The answer to that was Yes to the first question and No to the second.

Since this time, I have often used this trick to get fast energy when tired, and it works wonderfully.

If you are tapping trees for sap, which is bountiful in the spring, do re-member to say thank you by putting a plug in the hole where the sap was tapped. In that way, nothing will ever happen to the tree. If you are boiling down sap, remember it takes a lot to get a gallon of sugar syrup, but don't get discouraged because the reward is so great you forget all the trouble you had to collect the golden fluid.

HEMLOCK

HEMLOCK

(Tsuga canadensis)

The eastern hemlock is a medium-sized tree. The trunk is usually straight but much tapered from the base upwards. The branches are very slender and flexible. The leaves are the most reliable distinguishing feature. They are narrowly elongated, distinctly stalked, always appearing two-ranked.

The leaves are dark green and grooved above, marked with two white lines beneath. The fruit is a small, short-stalked cone, pale green at first and turning red-brown at maturity.

The bark is reddish or grayish-brown, deeply furrowed into broad ridges.

IN THE BUSH

I use the hemlock for a tea. By the way, this hemlock is the tree of the forest and not the deadly water hemlock.

As Tea: A very good tea can be made out of young hemlock needles by steeping them in a pot of hot water for about 10 minutes. This tea is a favorite drink among lumbermen.

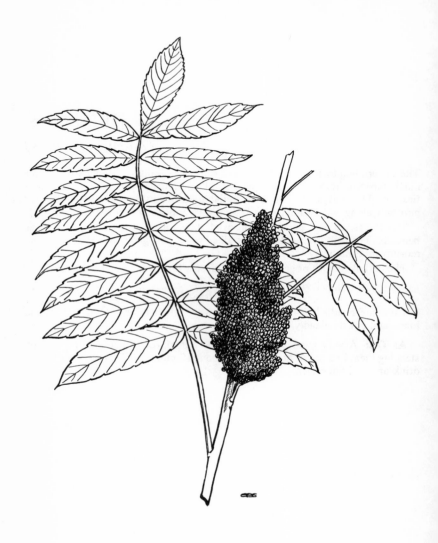

STAG SUMAC

STAG SUMAC

(Rhus typhina)

This tree or bush is easily recognized by its stout, velvety twigs, which resemble deer antlers that are still in velvet. The bark on these shrubs or small trees is smooth. The fernlike leaves, about 14 to 24 inches long, are composed of eleven to thirty-one pointed leaflets, from 2 to 5 inches in length. They are dark green on top and softly hairy beneath. The flowers are green in color and grow loosely in clusters.

This plant or tree seldom grows higher than 30 feet. It is apt to grow in clumps and has a tropical appearance with its long primate leaves turning to vivid yellow and crimson in the fall. Their autumnal beauty is further enhanced by torchlike panicles of fruit, small drupes matted together by the crimson plush of the hairs that cover them into pyramidal bunches terminating the branches. The sour taste of this fruit was used to advantage by the Indians and colonists to make a cooling drink. The crimson hairs yielded them a red dye when immersed in boiling water. Indians used the twigs, soaked, scraped, split and resoaked in water, to weave into baskets.

IN THE BUSH

The sumac is often called the lemonade tree or the vinegar tree.

As a Beverage: Many a time I have enjoyed the tart taste of sumac lemonade after a long and tiresome hike through the bush. Is is very simple to make. Pick over a couple of handfuls of the fruit. Crush the berries slightly, cover them with boiling water and let them steep away from the heat until the liquid is well colored. Sweeten to taste and serve cold.

The Indians used the shoots of the sumac as a **starvation food** when travelling in the early spring. The shoots are peeled and eaten raw.

They also made a **poultice** to put on irritated skin by bruising the leaves and the berries to a paste.

A **gargle,** made by boiling the crushed berries and leaves together in a small amount of water, is a good remedy for sore throats.

HOME RECIPES

SUMAC LEMONADE

5 pounds sumac berries	4 cups sugar
2 gallons water	2 lemons

Pick the berries over and discard any dark ones. In a large soup kettle boil the water. Add the sugar and stir, making sure all the sugar is dissolved. In another kettle crush the berries well with a large wooden spoon and add the peeled and quartered lemons. Pour the sugar and water solution over the berries and cover loosely with cheesecloth. Cool to room temperature. Clean the kettle you used for the water-sugar solution. Strain the berries through a large sieve into the second kettle and let stand overnight. Using an elastic, fasten a rubber or plastic hose to a stick which protrudes past the hose end. Place the protruding end on the kettle bottom, siphon off the lemonade into well-washed bottles, and refrigerate. The stick ensures that your hose is lifted free of any sediment at the bottom of the kettle.

SUMAC WINE

18 ounces dried sumac berries	2 Campden tablets
1 15-ounce package raisins	2 teaspoons yeast nutrient
5 pounds sugar	1 package wine yeast
2 gallons water	Wine-Art stabilizer tablets
2 teaspoons citric acid	

Boil the water in a large kettle. Mix all the ingredients except the yeast in a large primary fermenter. (I use a plastic wastebasket for this purpose). Add the water and stir with a large wooden spoon. When the must is cool (70° to 75°) sprinkle the yeast on top and cover with a plastic sheet. Let the mixture ferment for 6 or 7 days in a room with 70° temperature. Make a sugar solution of 2 parts sugar to 1 part water. On the fifth day add 2 cups of sugar solution, wait for 3 days and add 2 more cups. Strain the must through a large sieve and let stand for one day. Siphon the juice into 1 gallon jars and fit with fermentation locks. Rack in 3 weeks and again after 3 months. Bottle when the wine is clear and stable. Add 3 Wine-Art stabilizer tablets per gallon to prevent renewed fermentation.

BEARBERRY

(Arctostaphylos uva-ursi)

Bearberry is a trailing evergreen ground cover with hard red berries and small pink blossoms. The somewhat oval and shiny leaves are a dark green color. This plant is also called kinnickinnick.

The berries of this plant can be eaten but have a rather mealy taste. The first encounter I had with this plant was on a late summer night at a blue lake in northern Ontario. My Indian friend and I had finished a superb supper of fresh-caught speckled trout with arrowhead tubers, and now the old coffee pot was perking at the fireside. After a month in the wilderness, the tobacco supply was about to give out.

The only thing missing now, I told my friend, is a good smoke. He took a long look at me and then he set off into the bush. In a few minutes he was back with a handful of leaves which he placed on a flat stone to dry for a few minutes at the fireside. Then he crumbled up a few leaves and told me to try them in my pipe. They were raw and it took some time to get the pipe started, but after several attempts I finally had a smoke which at that time seemed

BEARBERRY

better than the finest cigar. Later I learned to collect these leaves, dry them thoroughly, and pulverize and mix them into regular tobacco.

In spring a sunny spot where this plant grows is a good place to look for bears because the black bear loves bearberry and it is one of the first things he will head for after he comes out of hibernation.

SUGAR MAPLE

SUGAR MAPLE

(Acer saccharum)

The maples are deciduous trees with opposite, simple or compound, variously lobed leaves, winter buds with few to many scales, and smooth or rough bark. All species have the terminal bud.

Maple sugar and maple syrup were two of the most welcome gifts the Indians presented to the white man. This stately tree, which can reach a height of 120 feet or more, yields from 3 to 6 pounds of sap every year and was a major source of sugar for the Indians. In the early spring when warm days succeeded by freezing nights arrive, the sap becomes active and starts to rise in the trunks. This is the time to harvest.

The Indians used to cut a V-shaped gash into the bark and at the point of the V they inserted a spout made from a hollow elder branch. The sap was collected in birch bark pails and baskets. About 2 gallons of sap every 24 hours is a normal yield from a tree. Remember to collect the sap as often as possible because the sap sours very rapidly if exposed to the sun.

The sap is boiled over a slow fire, and the scum is skimmed off the surface as it rises. The mixture is ready to pour into molds when it candies on the snow.

How much the Indians appreciated the maple sugar can be seen in old Indian molds, carved in wood, depicting the birds and the animals in the bush which were particularly wanted by Indians. The Ojibway Indians often made small birch bark cones to hold the sugar.

Maple syrup is made in the same way, except the sap is boiled for a shorter time and poured off before it becomes sugar.

You still can see maple sugar and maple syrup being made in the old-time sugaring huts in Ontario, Quebec and New England. It is an experience no child should miss because the method has changed very little in three centuries, and no one can resist the fun of this wonderful old custom.

IN THE BUSH

The uses of the maple sugar and syrup are endless as sweetening agents, quick energy foods or delicacies with a very special flavor of their own.

SUGAR PINE
(Pinus monticola)

This tree is also called western pine. It can reach a height of 250 feet. The needle-like leaves in bundles of 5 are stiff, 2 to 5 inches long and bluish-green. The fruit is a slender long-stalked, yellow-brown cone, 4 to 10 inches long with thin scales. The bark on young stems is silvery-gray, thin and smooth. On old trunks it is cinnamon-brown and broken into small, thick plates.

IN THE BUSH

The Indians used the sap as a sugar substitute. Injuries to the tree cause a bleeding of the sap, which forms large lumps of a white sugary substance when fresh. Many a time I have used this sap to sweeten my tea or coffee. The sap should be used with moderation, as it has a laxative quality.

SUGAR PINE

COLTSFOOT

(Tussilago farfara)

This plant is characterized by the flowers that bloom before the leaves appear. The flowers are yellow, and the leaves are all basal, large and round, with a heart-shaped base and lobed and toothed margins. The undersurface of the leaves is covered with a dense feltlike substance.

IN THE BUSH

Many a time, I am sure, you have been caught in the bush without salt. At least I have, and food tastes rather flat without it. But more than likely you have been as close to salt as the greens around you. The plant used by the Indians is the same plant which in England is called son-before-the-father. Of course the name means that the flowers appear before the leaves.

To Make Salt: To extract the salt, the Indians used to roll the green leaves into small balls and place them in the sun to dry.

After the leaves are dry (it takes from 4 to 5 days) the Indians placed the small balls on a flat stone and burned them until only ashes remained. The white ashes are very saline and make an excellent substitute for salt.

In fact, when you get used to this way of salting your food, it is hard to get used to ordinary salt again.

COLTSFOOT

WILD LEEK

WILD LEEK

(Allium tricoccum)

You will find the wild leek in early May, likely before the snow has melted from shaded places. Wandering in the bush in early spring when the earth still smells of rotten leaves and fresh spring water, you may come across a fragrant smell of onion.

More than likely you will be standing near a large patch of wild leek. Take advantage of your opportunity to collect this spring vegetable which, when used with moderation, is delightful in all salads.

This wild plant of the lily family is much stronger to the taste than the cultivated leek. The leaves, which appear in early spring before the flowers develop, are broadly elliptical.

On my early spring hikes in the bush, I usually carry with me a small plastic box filled with butter in case I come upon a patch of leeks.

IN THE BUSH

The whole plant can be eaten, either raw in a salad or cooked. My favorite recipe, however, is for spring leek soup.

HOME RECIPE

LEEK AND POTATO SOUP

2 quarts chicken stock	½ teaspoon pepper
4 cups peeled and coarsely chopped potatoes	1 cup heavy cream
3 cups leeks, sliced	3 tablespoons chives, finely chopped
1 teaspoon salt	

Using a soup kettle, bring the chicken stock to a boil. Lower the heat and add the potatoes, leeks and the salt and pepper. Simmer for 30 minutes.

Take the kettle off the heat and stir in the cream. Simmer for another 15 minutes but do not let the soup come to a boil.

Serve in individual soup bowls and sprinkle a little of the chives on top of each serving.

POISONOUS PLANTS

Many toxic plants have been used as poisons since early Greek times. A ruler afraid of being poisoned would have professional tasters to test his food and drink before he would touch them. Today, in the United States and Canada several people die every year from eating either poisonous mushrooms or plants. Most of these cases are accidental and could have been prevented with a little knowledge. Since it is almost impossible to learn to recognize the several thousand North American edible plants, in survival we find that it is much easier to learn what *not* to eat. It is the greatest thing to see families collecting wild edible plants on their outings together, but a word of warning. Teach your children as young as possible to recognize the plants and what they are used for. I remember many a walk in the bush with my father pointing out various plants and describing their use in survival. He took me on these nature trips during all seasons of the year.

Don't let fear of poisonous plants scare you away from gathering wild plants but prepare yourself to recognize the dangerous ones. An excellent way to do so is to gather drawings and descriptions of the plants and carry them with you on your trips into the woods. It won't take very long before you can make a positive identification and you will feel the satisfaction of being on the inside with Nature.

The following plants are among the most poisonous growing in North America.

MUSHROOMS

Sometimes known by the Latin name fungi, mushrooms are part of a large group of primitive organisms including also bacteria, algae and lichens, which comprise the division of the plant kingdom known as *Thallophyta*. Unlike algae and higher plants, the fungi lack chlorophyll, the green coloring matter of plants, and are therefore unable to make their own food. About 40,000 species of fungi have been described, and authorities have established that this figure represents only one-third of the total number in existence.

The fungus family has some very delicious edibles and some of the deadliest, so beware when using them for food. Some fungi are so deadly that just a few spores may poison fatally. In some instances there is no remedy known.

If you have to pick mushrooms and you know very little about them, here are a few rules written by one of the best-known experts on the subject.

1) Don't pick mushrooms in the button stage or any beginning to decay.

2) Don't pick those having "death cups" — stalks with swollen bases surrounded by saclike or scarred envelopes, especially if the underside is white.

3) Don't pick fungi having milky juice.

4) Don't pick fungi where the cap is thin in proportion to the gills and where the gills are nearly equal in length, especially if the cap is brightly colored.

5) Avoid all tube-bearing fungi.

6) Don't pick a fungus which has a web or ring around the upper part of the stem.

An old misconception is that boiling or soaking the mushroom will cause the poison to disappear, and the mushroom will be edible. This is far from the truth, and has brought many people to the hospital or the graveyard.

If you are not sure of the identification of a fungus, leave it alone. The effect of the poison does not show until it has begun its deadly work on nerve centers, and the unfortunate victim is beyond help.

If there is any suspicion that poisonous toadstools have been eaten, send for a doctor at once and tell him what the trouble is so that he can bring a hypodermic syringe and atropine sulphate. In the meantime, give the victim an emetic of 4 to 7 glassfuls of lukewarm water or milk. You can mix soapsuds into the water if you wish.

Among the deadliest mushrooms are the **fly amanita** and **deadly amanita**. Called the destroying angel, the first is brownish yellow or white. The second varies from pink, brown, yellow or reddish in the center shading to a pale yellow at the edges. All have white gills, a ringlike collar on the stem and a cup at the base.

FLY AMANITA   DEADLY AMANITA

BUTTERCUP   JIMSON WEED

BUTTERCUP

The common buttercup contains an acrid volatile anemonin, which is sometimes strong enough to raise blisters on the skin. Internally, a severe inflam-
mation of the intestines may develop. Being volatile, the poison is driven off
by drying.

JIMSON WEED

The name jimson weed is a contraction from "Jamestown weed", a name
given by early colonists who found the plant growing near Jamestown, Virginia.
Like many members of the *Datura* family, it is very poisonous and has a long
history as a medicine. Jimson weed is an annual and is over 4 feet tall, with
ovate, unevenly toothed, smooth, strongly scented leaves, white or purplish
funnel-shaped flowers, and hard, prickly many-seeded capsules splitting into
4 valves.

Its poisonous properties are due to the presence of alkaloids throughout the
entire plant, mainly scopolamine, but also hyoscyamine. The roots usually
contain the smallest quantity of these, and the leaves and seeds normally contain the largest. Both alkaloids are used in the treatment of nervous disorders.

This plant promises to become a commercial source of scopolamine, which
is now being used as a pre-anesthetic in surgery and childbirth, in opthal-
mology, and for the prevention of motion sickness.

POISON IVY *(Rhus radicans)*

Most of us have been in contact with poison ivy or been victims of it, but
many of us would not recognize the plant even if we placed the picnic cloth on
top of it. This plant may appear as a shrubby plant only a few inches high and
carpeting the ground, or as an upright plant 2 to 3 feet tall, or it may become

177

vinelike, twining itself around trees, shrubs and posts and reaching some distance from the ground.

Leaves of the poison ivy consist of 3 leaflets. The stalk of the middle leaflet is longer than the stalks of the 2 side leaflets. All 3 stalks are joined together at the upper end of one much longer stalk, the petiole, which grows out from a bud on the woody stem. The color changes from early spring's deep green to summer's bright green. The upper surface of the leaves is nearly smooth and sometimes has a glossy appearance. No definite shape can be assigned to the leaflets, for they vary greatly in shape and size. The underside of the leaflets may be finely hairy all over or may be virtually without hairs. In the spring, small clusters of erect, greenish-white flowers develop in the angles where the leaf petioles join the stem. The flowers are often hidden by the leaves. During the summer these flowers develop small, round hard berries about ¼ inch in diameter. After the leaves have dropped in the fall, poison ivy can be identified easily by the clusters of grayish to white waxy-looking berries on bare stems with alternate buds and leaf scars.

Poison ivy has a distressing toxic action on the skin of people who become sensitized to it. The offending substance is an oil which is present throughout root, stem, leaf, flower and fruit. The tearing or bruising of any part liberates the oil, which may come into contact with exposed parts of the body, either directly or by handling contaminated objects. The oil may stick to clothing, boots, tools or picnic baskets and can be easily transferred to hands and thence to the face or by handclasp to others who have not been directly exposed.

If contact with this plant or with an article thought to be contaminated has occurred, the advice of a doctor should be sought. If a physician is not available, wash the oil from the skin by repeated thorough lathering with soap accompanied by generous rinsings of water.

POISON IVY

Once the blisters have appeared, rubbing should be carefully avoided. Irritation at this stage may be relieved by the application of cloths wrung from ice water or by cool baths containing Epsom salts, starch, baking soda or boracic acid. The application of oily or greasy ointments or liniments should be avoided.

Clothing contaminated by poison ivy should be thoroughly and repeatedly washed with soap and water or dry-cleaned. If you send it to the dry-cleaners, put it into a plastic bag and mark it "contaminated by poison ivy". The oil will remain on the clothing for an indefinite period, and such clothing subsequently worn or handled by any other individual may cause active ivy poisoning.

POISON OAK   POISON SUMAC

POISON OAK *(Rhus diversiloba)*

This plant is found on the Pacific slopes of the United States and Canada. The leaves are more rounded, less pointed, or more abruptly pointed than the poison ivy or poison sumac. The plant resembles poison ivy and has the same potential.

Treatment of the skin rash caused by the plant is the same as for poison ivy and poison sumac.

POISON SUMAC *(Rhus vernix)*

The poison sumac differs from the non-poison sumac in that it grows on marshy ground. Its leaflets are not sharply toothed, the inflorescences are drooping or spreading, the fruits whitish and smooth. The treatment of rashes from poison sumac is the same as for poison ivy. The early settlers made a paste out of soap and water about the consistency of lard which they applied thickly on the irritated spot and left overnight.

These three plants are not edible, and care should be taken to avoid them because all the fun of collecting edible plants is gone if you have a bad case of ivy poisoning.

POKEWEED

Pokeweed is a strong-smelling perennial herb. The plant is from 3 to 12 feet tall, bears smooth, entire leaves and long racemes of small flowers followed by dark purple berries which ripen in the fall. The young shoots and seedlings are often harmful. The root is very poisonous. The deep crimson juice, formerly used to tint wine or preserves, also has poisonous qualities. The name comes from the Indian *pocan*, a dye-yielding plant, but the color is not fast and is otherwise unfit for dyeing.

The use of pokeweed as rural medicine has been wholly abandoned because of many poisonings.

POKEWEED

WATER HEMLOCK (*Cicuta*)

This deadly plant is known under many names in different parts of the country, such as beaver poison, spotted parsley, muskrat weed, and musquash root. The last two names are inspired by the muskrat, which inhabits such swamps as the *Cicuta* affects; and the odor of the roots of certain species of *Cicuta* also recalls the musk-scented rodent.

The plant stands 3 to 6 feet in height, with a rigid hollow stem marked with purple lines or spots, and grows in water. The leaves are decompound or even three-pinnate, having coarsely serrate leaflets, with veins apparently ending in notches instead of at the points of the teeth as in ordinary foliage. The flowers are very tiny and white, in decompound terminal umbels, with stalks of unequal length. The fruits are oblong, smooth and slightly flattened laterally. Spindle-shaped tuberous roots cluster about the base of the stem, and are the cause of many deaths.

These roots have an aromatic flavor and fresh substance and are frequently mistaken for the roots of parsnips, artichokes or even horse radish. Even livestock are sometimes killed by feeding on them or by drinking water poisoned by roots which have been crushed under the cattle's hooves. The poisonous element in this plant is an oily fluid. This fluid is found throughout the plant but chiefly in the roots. When eaten, *Cicuta* produces vomiting, colic, staggering and unconsciousness, and finally, frightful convulsions which end in death.

No chemical antidote being known, the only treatment possible is to cleanse the digestive system thoroughly. Learn to recognize this plant — it is essential for all people who like to collect wild edible plants.

A drink made by brewing its brother the poison hemlock is said to have been the instrument used in old Athens for the execution of criminals. This drink was probably the cause of Socrates' death.

WATER HEMLOCK

WHITE SNAKEROOT *(Eupatorium rugosum)*

In Lincoln's time milk sickness was a common aliment, but only recently was white snakeroot discovered to be the cause. White snakeroot contains a poison, tremetol, which is soluble in butterfat or milk and may be transmitted through them to humans or animals.

The plant grows 3 to 4 feet tall, has oval, coarsely serrated leaves, and corymbs of white flowers. It is widespread in woods and clearings.

This plant has earned a reputation as a folk medicine for breaking up fevers. Tradition has it that eupatorium is good for broken bones (the common name "boneset" preserves this notion). It has no such action. By reason of a certain amount of volatile and fixed oil which eupatorium contains, it makes a fair diaphoretic, or perspiration-producing, mixture, and in the form of "boneset tea" it is of service in causing profuse sweating.

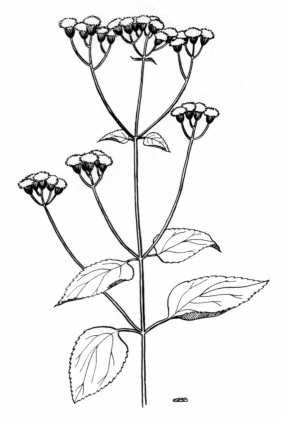

WHITE SNAKEROOT

INDEX

WILD EDIBLE PLANTS IN THEIR SEASONS

SPRING RECIPES

Dandelion	Stinging Nettle	Wild Onion
Great Burdock	Thistle	Strawberry (leaves)
Milkweed	Watercress	Black Birch
Mint	Yellow Clover	Bearberry
Ostrich Fern	Jerusalem Artichoke	Sugar Maple

SUMMER RECIPES

Black Mustard	Purslane	Elderberry (flowers)
Chickweed	Sheep Sorrel	Raspberry (berries)
Common Plantain	Thistle	Strawberry (berries)
Dandelion	Watercress	Wild Rose
Evening Primrose	Wood Sorrel	Black Birch
Great Burdock	Yellow Clover	Bearberry
Lamb's-Quarters	Jerusalem Artichoke	Coltsfoot
Milkweed	Wild Onion	
Mint	Yellow Waterlily	

FALL RECIPES

Black Mustard	Jerusalem Artichoke	Strawberry (leaves)
Chickweed	Yellow Waterlily	Chokecherry
Common Plantain	Beaked Hazelnut	Wild Rose
Lamb's-Quarters	Chestnut	Stag Sumac
Mint	Wild Rice	Bearberry
Sheep Sorrel	Elderberry (berries)	Coltsfoot
Watercress	Raspberry (leaves)	

ALL-YEAR RECIPES

Bulrush	Wintergreen	Hemlock
Cattail	Arrowhead	Sugar Pine